First World War
and Army of Occupation
War Diary
France, Belgium and Germany

52 DIVISION
157 Infantry Brigade
Highland Light Infantry
5th (City of Glasgow) Battalion (Territorial)
30 July 1917 - 5 May 1919

WO95/2898/2

The Naval & Military Press Ltd
www.nmarchive.com
Published in association with The National Archives

Published by

The Naval & Military Press Ltd

Unit 10 Ridgewood Industrial Park,

Uckfield, East Sussex,

TN22 5QE England

Tel: +44 (0) 1825 749494

www.naval-military-press.com

www.nmarchive.com

This diary has been reprinted in facsimile from the original. Any imperfections are inevitably reproduced and the quality may fall short of modern type and cartographic standards.

© **Crown Copyright**
Images reproduced by permission of The National Archives, London, England, 2015.

Contents

Document type	Place/Title	Date From	Date To
Heading	WO95/2898-2		
Heading	52nd Division 157th Infy Bde 1-5th Bn Highland Lt Infy Apr 1918-May 1919		
Heading	157th Brigade 52nd Division Disembarked Marseilles From Egypt 17.4.18 1/5th Battalion Highland Light Infantry April 1918		
Heading	Vol I 5th H.L.I War Diary April 1918 Vol 34		
War Diary	Castle Hill	01/04/1918	02/04/1918
War Diary	Sarona	03/04/1918	03/04/1918
War Diary	Surafend	04/04/1918	06/04/1918
War Diary	Kantara	07/04/1918	07/04/1918
War Diary	Sidi Bishr	08/04/1918	10/04/1918
War Diary	At Sea	11/04/1918	17/04/1918
War Diary	Marseille	18/04/1918	19/04/1918
War Diary	In Train	20/04/1918	22/04/1918
War Diary	St. Valery	23/04/1918	28/04/1918
War Diary	Berguette	29/04/1918	29/04/1918
War Diary	La Lacque	30/04/1918	30/04/1918
Miscellaneous	1/5th Battalion Highland Light Infantry Nominal Roll of Officers		
Miscellaneous	1/5th Battalion Highland Light Infantry Nominal Roll		
Heading	1/5th H.L.I. War Diary May 1918 Vol XXXVI		
War Diary	La Lacque	01/05/1918	06/05/1918
War Diary	Neuville St Vaast	07/05/1918	07/05/1918
War Diary	Vimy	08/05/1918	24/05/1918
War Diary	Mt St Eloi	25/05/1918	31/05/1918
Heading	5th H.L.I. War Diary June 1918 Vol 37		
War Diary	Mt St Eloy	01/06/1918	01/06/1918
War Diary	Willerval	02/06/1918	22/06/1918
War Diary	Neuville St Vaast	23/06/1918	29/06/1918
War Diary	Vimy	30/06/1918	30/06/1918
Operation(al) Order(s)	5th Battalion Highland Light Infantry Order No. 3	01/06/1918	01/06/1918
Miscellaneous	5th Battn H.L.I. Warning Order No. 8	12/06/1918	12/06/1918
Operation(al) Order(s)	5th Bn. H.L.I. Order No. 9	18/06/1918	18/06/1918
Operation(al) Order(s)	5th Bn. H.L.I. Order No. 10	18/06/1918	18/06/1918
Miscellaneous	5th H.L.I. Administrative Instructions For Order No. 10	27/06/1918	27/06/1918
Heading	5th Bn H.L.I. War Diary No.38 Volume I July 1918		
War Diary	Vimy	01/07/1918	16/07/1918
War Diary	Fraser Camp St. Eloy	17/07/1918	20/07/1918
War Diary	Lozinghem	21/07/1918	29/07/1918
War Diary	Bois D'Olhain Barlin	30/07/1917	30/07/1917
War Diary	Ecurie Wood Camp Near Roclincourt	31/07/1917	31/07/1917
Operation(al) Order(s)	5th H.L.I. Order No. 11	03/07/1918	03/07/1918
Heading	5 H.L.I. Appendix & War Diary For July 1915		
Operation(al) Order(s)	5th H.L.I. Order No. 12	04/07/1918	04/07/1918
Operation(al) Order(s)	5th H.L.I. Order No. 13	15/07/1918	15/07/1918
Miscellaneous	5th H.L.I. Administrative Instructions To Order No. 13	15/07/1918	15/07/1918
Operation(al) Order(s)	5th H.L.I. Order No. 14	24/07/1918	24/07/1918
Miscellaneous	Reference Order No. 14	24/07/1918	24/07/1918
Miscellaneous	5th Battn. H.L.I. Reference Order No. 14 Para 3	24/07/1918	24/07/1918

Operation(al) Order(s)	5th H.L.I. Order No. 15	29/07/1918	29/07/1918
Heading	5th H.L.I War Diary Volume 39 August 1918		
War Diary	Longwood	01/08/1918	10/08/1918
War Diary	Line	11/08/1918	16/08/1918
War Diary	Chateau De La Haie	17/08/1918	20/08/1918
War Diary	Agnez Les Duisans	21/08/1918	22/08/1918
War Diary	Bellacourt	23/08/1918	28/08/1918
War Diary	Mercatel	29/08/1918	31/08/1918
Operation(al) Order(s)	5th Battn H.L.I. Order No. 16	06/08/1918	06/08/1918
Operation(al) Order(s)	5th Bn H.L.I. Order No. 17	07/08/1918	07/08/1918
Miscellaneous	Reference Battalion Order No. 17	07/08/1918	07/08/1918
Operation(al) Order(s)	5th Battn. H.L.I. Order No. 16	08/08/1918	08/08/1918
Operation(al) Order(s)	5th Bn. H.L.I. Order No. 19	11/08/1918	11/08/1918
Miscellaneous	5th Battn H.L.I. Warning Order No. 23	21/08/1918	21/08/1918
Operation(al) Order(s)	157th Infantry Brigade Order No. 130	24/08/1918	24/08/1918
Operation(al) Order(s)	157th Bde. Order No. 135	27/08/1918	27/08/1918
Operation(al) Order(s)	5th H.L.I. Order No. 20	15/08/1918	15/08/1918
Operation(al) Order(s)	5th H.L.I. Order No. 21	17/08/1918	17/08/1918
Map	German Trenches In Blue		
Map	Map		
Heading	57b. N.W. No.2 C.O		
War Diary	Mercatel	01/09/1918	02/09/1918
War Diary	Bullecourt	02/09/1918	03/09/1918
War Diary	Near Inchy	04/09/1918	13/09/1918
War Diary	St. Leger	14/09/1918	17/09/1918
War Diary	Near Moeuvres	18/09/1918	19/09/1918
War Diary	Noreuil	20/09/1918	30/09/1918
Heading	57c N.E. 1/20000		
Map	Map		
Heading	57c N.E. 1/20000		
Heading	1/5th H.L.I. Oct 1918		
Heading	War Diary 1/5th Battalion Highland Light Infantry October 1918		
War Diary	S.W.Of Cambrai	01/10/1918	05/10/1918
War Diary	E. 26 W. of Canal Du Nord	06/10/1918	07/10/1918
War Diary	Lignereuil	08/10/1918	20/10/1918
War Diary	Henin-Lietard Planque	21/10/1918	24/10/1918
War Diary	Flines	25/10/1918	26/10/1918
War Diary	Landas	27/10/1918	27/10/1918
War Diary	Lucelles	28/10/1918	31/10/1918
War Diary	Lecelles	01/11/1918	03/11/1918
War Diary	St Amand	04/11/1918	07/11/1918
War Diary	Odomez	08/11/1918	08/11/1918
War Diary	Harchies	09/11/1918	09/11/1918
War Diary	Gapennes	10/11/1918	10/11/1918
War Diary	W Of Mons	11/11/1918	12/11/1918
War Diary	Erbisoeuil	13/11/1918	31/01/1919
Miscellaneous	Extraction Slip		
War Diary	Erbisoeul	01/02/1919	13/03/1919
War Diary	Maizieres	14/03/1919	20/03/1919
War Diary	Soignies	21/03/1919	31/03/1919
Miscellaneous	To 52nd Division	08/04/1919	08/04/1919
Miscellaneous	To 157th Inf. Bde.	30/05/1919	30/05/1919
War Diary	Soignies	01/04/1919	28/04/1919
War Diary	Dunkirk	29/04/1919	03/05/1919
War Diary	Southampton	04/05/1919	05/05/1919

WD95/2898(2)

WD95/2898(2)

52ND DIVISION
157TH INFY BDE

1-5TH BN HIGHLAND LT INFY

APR 1918-MAY 1919

157th Brigade.
52nd Division.

Disembarked MARSEILLES from EGYPT 17.4.18.

1/5th BATTALION

HIGHLAND LIGHT INFANTRY

APRIL 1918.

5th H.L.I.

WAR DIARY

April 1918

Vol 34

WAR DIARY
or
INTELLIGENCE SUMMARY.
(Erase heading not required.)

Army Form C. 2118.

34/1

Place	Date	Hour	Summary of Events and Information	Remarks and references to Appendices
Castle Hill	1st April 18		Carried out Tactical Scheme attacking position by 2 battalions. Subsequently we picked ourselves from our officers. Just before rifle drill of 9/10 Pl: Advance party under Lt Turnbull left for Sarona, at	
"	2nd Ap.		O.C. 1/8th Gurkhas came up to look at position. 1/8 Gurkhas secured in camp 2115. Bn. Hands over & left Sarona area at 2130 at arriving in Sarona 0100. 3rd April. Officers went into billets. O.R.s bivouaced at.	
Sarona	3rd Ap.		Bn. left Sarona with remainder 157 Brigade & marched to Ludd when the 52nd Division had been ordered to concentrate. Head of column left Sarona 1830 and arrived at Surafend Camp near LUDD 22.15 at	
Surafend	4		Battalion hutted in store ? to Ordnance. Lt. J. Girvan rejoined from hospital. 2nd Lieut Williamson from El Arish School returns to Regt. Lieut General Allenby C. in C. rode round the Camp. T Lieut F.C.Wylie R.A.M.C. joined the Battalion as medical officer vice Lieut P. Stewart, who transferred to 1/6th Essex Regiment	

A 5834 Wt. W.4973/M687. 750,000. 8/16 D.D. & L. Ltd. Forms/C.2118/13.

WAR DIARY
or
INTELLIGENCE SUMMARY

Army Form C. 2118.

34/2.

Place	Date	Hour	Summary of Events and Information	Remarks and references to Appendices
SURAFEND	5th April 10½	3.30 pm	Remained in Camp. Completed handing over of kits & drew stores from Ordnance at 23.00.	
" "	6th April		Battalion entrained at JUDD at 08.00 for Kantara & arrived there 23.00.	
KANTARA	7th		Lieut W.H. Milne & 2 Lieut J. Filchner reported from 1st I.B.D. vice 2nd Lieut McSteavy & 2nd Lieut T.F. Murray who returned to 1 I.B.D. Kantara. Draft of 38 O.R. joined from 1st I.B.D. Field Postal Staff proceeded to Jaffa as evidence. G.C.M. Battalion 40 Officers 1011 O.R. entrained at 20.00 for Sidi Bishr (Alexandria) at	
SIDI BISHR	8th		Arriving Sidi Bishr 06.30. Went into rest camp, only 10% allowed on pass to Alexandria.	
SIDI BISHR	9th		Battalion received orders to entrain 10.30 for the docks. Train was 4½ hours late by Bn was entrained in 15 minutes. Staff left for Schoura tome, left at Schoura tome, Argyles (men than Wilson) (also to return to camp. In meantime camp occupied by other troops. Bivouacked	

WAR DIARY
or
INTELLIGENCE SUMMARY.

Army Form C. 2118.

34/3

Place	Date	Hour	Summary of Events and Information	Remarks and references to Appendices
SIDI BISHR	10th April 1918		Battalion again entrained, this time 0650 proceeded to Alexandria docks & embarked on H.M.T. Omrah. R.E. & Lowland Field Ambulance on board. Battalion 40 officers (incl. Docks & Padre) & 10 11 other ranks.	per appendix no. 1. nominal roll
AT SEA	11th April		Found out from the Docks at 0700. Sailed at 1400 &	
"	12th "			
"	13th "		At Sea. Physical training, boat drill, lectures etc. O.C.	
"	14th "			
"	15th "			
"	16th "			
"	17th "		Arrived Marseilles 0830. Battalion disembarked 40 officers O.R at 1400 and marched to Camp no. 10 (Huntzner) pouring rain & all ranks were soaked through. Arrived in camp 1645. 20 pairs socks 2/C issued	
MARSEILLES	18th "		Remained in No 10 Camp Marseilles. 10% pairs issued & men to town. Of	

Army Form C. 2118.

WAR DIARY
or
INTELLIGENCE SUMMARY.
(Erase heading not required.)

Army Form C. 2118.

34/4

Place	Date	Hour	Summary of Events and Information	Remarks and references to Appendices
MARSEILLES	19th April		Battalion 40 officers & 1001 O.R. entrained at Marseilles & left at 1047 for North of France	
In train	20th	"	Battalion remained on train. Halt spent at Le Teil 1200. AL	
"	21st	"	Battn on train. Halt spent 0200 at PARAY-LE-MONAIL. Halt spent at MALESHERBES 1200. Had dinners	MALESHERBES 1200
"	22nd	"	Battalion arrived at NOYELLE-SUR-MER at 1230 & detrained. At NOYELLE & left there at 1630 for ST VALERIE-SUR-SOMME. Arrived there 1800 & went into billets. Lt Col J.B. Nelson DSO reported from leave & assumed Command of the Battalion. AL Battalion detrained 40 officers 998 O.R. Battn went into billets which were poor & dirty. FULL	
ST VALARY	23rd		Inspected billets. Companies busy making up lists of deficiences. All Companies	
	24th		All Companies training - paying particular attention to gas training. All Companies medically inspected - 27% found to be in a venereous condition. Capt. MORRISON, STRACHAN & MAIN & Lt T.B. CLARKE returned from Home leave. The following changes made in Companies: Capt. MORRISON to command D Coy. Vice Capt.	

WAR DIARY
or
INTELLIGENCE SUMMARY
(Erase heading not required.)

Army Form C. 2118.

34/5

S.H.1

Place	Date	Hour	Summary of Events and Information	Remarks and references to Appendices
ST VALERY	24/4/18		Capt L.H. WATSON 1/c 2nd i/Command of D Coy. Capt MAPP to be 2nd i/Command of A Coy vice Lt J.M. PIPER to be Batt Lewis Gun Officer. Capt STRACHAN to be 2nd i/c of C Coy vice Capt MILLER to 2nd i/c of B Coy vice Lt CARMICHAEL to Command H.Q. of C Coy vice Capt MILLER to 2nd i/c of B Coy vice 2nd/Lt HARISON of B Coy appointed Batt Gas Officer & transferred to a Platoon. 2nd/Lt HARISON of B Coy appointed Batt Gas Officer & transferred to H.Qrs Coy. The following transport drawn at ABBEVILLE. 10 G.S. Limbers, 4 Kitchens, 2 water Carts, 1 medical Cart, 1 machine Cart. 8 H.D. Horses, 26 L.D. Horses. 2 Platoons of C. Coy moved to new billets on account of overcrowded state of their present billets Pell.	FRANCE ABBEVILLE 1/100000
	25/4/18		25 officers & N.C.O's attended gas Lecture by Gas Officer in Cples. Projected new transport in afternoon. Drew 4 more Lewis Guns & drivers for use with Batt. Scouts. Day fine but cold. Fell.	
	26/4/18		G.O.C. Division paid a visit. Parade of Battn ordered by Bde. Cnt Battn not inspected by G.O.C. Informed that Bde would probably move on 28th inst. to 1st Army area. Group of officers taken at L'ABBAYE. Inspected the 4 new Lewis Guns. Yorka to all N.C.O of Battn. Concert in the Evening Pell.	
	27/4/18		Advance party for billeting of 1 officer (2/Lt TURNBULL) 48 O/Rs left for new area.	

WAR DIARY
or
INTELLIGENCE SUMMARY

Army Form C. 2118.

5th H.L.I.

Place	Date	Hour	Summary of Events and Information	Remarks and references to Appendices
ST. VALERY	27/4/18		Inspected billets - very clean & in good order. Coys training. Weather fine hot. Cold. Drew from transport - 2 Adies; 1 Sau H.D, 2 Shaves H.D, 7 Picks. Received orders to move to new area & Thornwood Seam with O.C. Coys. held.	
	28/4/18		Moved to new area:	
		1530	D Coy + Major BEARD with 1 field kitchen left for entrainment at NOYELLES at 1814.	
		1630	Transport left billets for NOYELLES.	
		1830	Batt. less D Coy. left for NOYELLES arriving at 2000 - not entrained - 40 7/80 to a truck. Much stagging on bus & march. Hill.	
BERGUETTE	29/4/18	0045	arrived at BERGUETTE. Detrained and marched to huts at LA LACQUE, arriving at 0700. Lay about on settling down. Men feet inspected. Huts cleared. Fair weather. Many fumes heard all day to the East.	
LA LACQUE	30/4/18		Very wet wet morning. At 0900 went with O.C. + other C.O. to see line which to being dug running N-South from P.21.C.87 to B.01.3 at present at J.20.d.22 5th H.L.I. allotted the right sub section of the line. From P.21.C.87 (85 to J.32 a 30 ox). Afternoon went carefully over this line with Major CRAWFORD totally over Officers & prepared & sent to Bde Scheme of defence. Besides holding the line the Batt. has to find various garrisons for all bridges across the L.V.S. CANAL between P.4 Central + J.26 Central. Lt CARMICHAEL reconnoitred the part of the Canal + reported c-bridges. Conferences Training Musketry Gas Masks.	France. Shadrah Shallies

1/5th BATTALION HIGHLAND LIGHT INFANTRY.

NOMINAL ROLL OF OFFICERS.

Major	Craufurd, A.	(Gordon Hldrs)	2/Lieut.	Nicolson, M.D.	(9-H.L.I.)
"	Brand, D.E.		"	Fraser, S.M.	(7-H.L.I.)
Capt. and Adjt.	Girot, H.A.		"	Hardie, J.L.	(9-H.L.I.)
Capt.	Parr, H.W.	(3rd H.L.I.)	"	MacKenzie, J.G.	
"	Currie, A.B.		"	Wright, J.B.	(9-H.L.I.)
"	Fyfe, T.A.		"	Penman, A.	(")
"	Moir, J.F.		"	Turnbull, R.	(")
"	Miller, R.M.		"	Todd, M.G.	(")
Lieut.	Watson, E.H.		"	Hillson, L.S.	(6-H.L.I.)
"	Carmichael, I.	(14-H.L.I.)	"	Cotterell, W.R.	
"	Parr, J.W.	(3rd H.L.I.)	"	Allison, T.A.	
"	Sweet, R.L.		"	McKie, J.	
"	Cumming, W.		"	Park, R.	
"	Legate, F.		"	Turner, E.D.	
"	Malcolm, A.H.	(9-H.L.I.)	"	Sanderson, C.M.	
"	Thomson, G.L.	(6-H.L.I.)	"	Brodie, C.F.	(9-H.L.I.)
"	Girvan, J.		"	Williamson, E.T.	
"	Milne, W.H.		"	Robertson, J.B.	
2/Lieut.	Shedden, J.		Lieut.	MacKenzie, R.N.	(R.A.M.C.)
"	Gilchrist, J.	(7-H.L.I.)	Rev.	Fuller, F.C.	(C.F.)

1/5th BATTALION HIGHLAND LIGHT INFANTRY.

NOMINAL ROLL.

"A" COY.

No.	Rank	Name
200139,	C.S.M.	Armour, J.
200041,	C.Q.M.S.	Holman, R.S.
200165,	L/C.	Currie, J.
200118,	Pte.	Callander, A.
35683,	"	Currie, S.L.
201287,	"	Gormley, J.
201232,	"	Gow, J.
201705,	"	Howie, J.
200496,	"	Inglis, D.
201182,	"	Wilson, W.
37479,	"	Wilson, R.
200106,	Bugler	Hargan, J.
200435,	Pte.	Lawrence, T.
201345,	"	McDevitt, J.
201387,	"	McKinlay, A.
200480,	"	Pollock, H.
200207,	"	McFarlane, G.
201108,	"	Dowds, J.
201582,	"	Frood, A.
201241,	"	Wilson, J.
201958,	"	Blair, J.
30168,	"	Cameron, A.
200698,	"	Roy, W.
201124,	"	Darroch, J.
200295,	Sergt.	Logan, J.
30512,	Corpl.	Marshall, P.
201546,	Pte.	Inglis, R.
37757,	"	McCLYmont, J.
30573,	"	Davie, J.
201435,	"	Ellison, W.
200115,	"	Bennet, A.
300206,	"	McKay, H.
200272,	L/C	McNulty, W.
201246,	Pte.	Marshall, J.
200396,	"	Budge, J.
201114,	"	Duffy, T.
203518,	Corpl.	O'Donnell, J.
200124,	L/C.	Rodgers, R.
29921,	Pte.	Fraser, W.S.
202200,	"	Robinson, J.
29690,	"	Whyte, A.
29790,	"	Broadfoot, W.
50166,	"	Ross, W.
203270,	"	Kane, P.
201358,	"	Meek, A.
32634,	"	McQueen, R.
200682,	"	McCafferty, T.
201243,	"	Gillies, L.
30516,	"	Hunter, A.
4953,	"	McFarlane, J.
29497,	"	Mabon, T.
29140,	"	Wallace, J.S.
38906,	"	Davidson, R.
29703,	"	Douglas, G.
50091,	"	Robertson, D.
200450,	"	Inglis, D.L.
201261,	"	Bryson, J.
282421,	"	Scott, W.
203270,	"	Stirling, W.
203275,	"	Baillie, J.
203688,	"	Dickson, J.
200166,	L/C.	McElwee, M.
31819,	Pte.	Marshall, R.
200618,	"	Brigg, G.
30496,	"	Hopper, G.
9208,	"	Petrie, J.
8608,	"	McNeill, A.
201044,	"	Campbell, J.
9203,	"	Noon, J.
200126,	L/Sgt.	McDougall, A.
200394,	Pte.	Campbell, W.L.
36339,	"	Boyle, J.
42021,	"	Ferguson, H.
5173,	"	Moir, T.
26167,	"	Porter, D.
201090,	"	Reid, W.
33405,	"	Scott, T.
21277,	"	Jeffrey, G.
203269,	"	Bulmer, A.
200228,	"	Darroch, K.
29719,	"	Black, W.
331509,	"	Mitchell, W.A.
201360,	"	Chilton, J.
200852,	"	Naismith, J.
33183,	"	Sweeney, R.
7738,	"	Logan, R.
28895,	"	Butler, R.
9105,	"	Gowie, A.
36023,	"	Ponsonby, J.
201611,	"	Anderson, N.
201100,	"	McGee, A.
201265,	"	Archer, T.
201179,	"	Henderson, G.
28793,	"	Gladstone, A.
200232,	"	Brookmyre, J.
1502,	"	Mackie, R.
200037,	Sergt.	Bain, A.
200312,	Corpl.	Urquhart, D.
282303,	Pte.	Bramley, W.
29579,	"	Taylor, J.
200571,	"	Hutton, J.
201003,	"	Feeney, D.
201341,	"	Spratt, J.
36320,	"	Graham, E.S.
32375,	"	Diamond, A.
200485,	"	Milwain, T.
200807,	"	Kelly, J.
203278,	"	Moran, T.
29343,	"	Graham, J.
30550,	"	Watson, M.
9484,	"	Roy, J.
202146,	"	Elliot, J.
203412,	"	Hunt, J.
29763,	"	Scott, T.C.
201586,	"	Carruthers, F.
32636,	"	Gibson, A.
38518,	"	Kane, J.
28905,	"	Hamilton, R.
201427,	"	Bradley, J.
201272,	"	Neill, J.
200348,	"	O'May, D.
200027,	Sergt?	Sykes, W.

201712,	Sergt.	Rowlinson, W.	26429,	Corpl.	Stewart, J.
200667,	Pte.	Richardson, P.	200886,	Pte.	Kinney, W.
201709,	"	Stafford, J.	201001,	"	Logan, T.
55888,	"	Lawrie, A.	28192,	"	Allan, D.
55800,	"	Lyall, G.	50572,	"	Craig, D.
50571,	"	Leckie, J.	27676,	"	Dinning, W.
200939,	L/C.	Pirie, G.	200222,	"	Buchanan, J.
200436,	Pte.	Gordon, A.	200826,	"	Smith, A.
201519,	"	Whitelaw, W.	55726,	"	Low, A.
202197,	"	Milne, W.	200411,	"	Burden, J.
201373,	"	Gormley, T.	27355,	L/C.	Moore, W.
243032,	"	McKenzie, D.	200453,	Pte.	Towers, T.
55831,	Pte.	Cairns, J.	200695,	"	Callan, E.
200996,	"	Cook, T.	200171,	"	Christie, A.
200181,	Sergt.	McLean, C.	55791,	"	Hagan, J.
36280,	Pte.	Taylor, W.	34975,	"	Loughery, J.
40132,	"	Vallance, D.	27232,	"	Maxwell, J.
201704,	"	Harvey, W.	201344,	"	Logan, J.
201510,	"	O'Donnell, T.	200212,	"	Overy, A.
201710,	"	Ridge, J.	201205,	"	Snodgrass, W.
200059,	"	Muir, W.E.	207701,	Sergt.	Jacobs, J.
50570,	L/C/	Gearty, F.	200881,	Pte.	Graham, A.M.
203061,	Pte.	Dorrien, T.	2274,	"	Hainning, R.
1153,	"	Somerville, N.	21136,	"	Spedding, W.
201512,	"	Mair, H.	29633,	"	Henderson, J.G.
200140,	"	Doleman, T.	201340,	"	Darroch, D.
200577,	"	McLean, D.	200268,	Corpl.	Cameron, J.
201518,	"	Hillson, J.	24213,	Pte.	King, G.
200701,	"	Nisbet, H.	200342,	"	Murphy, W.
200267,	"	McColl, J.	20584,	"	Bolland, C.
201706,	"	Smail, P.	201301,	"	Fletcher, P.
200946,	Sergt.	Creek, J.	61193,	L/C.	McCarroll, J.
46200,	Pte.	Edwards, S.	29888,	Pte.	Brown, J.
28263,	"	Howard, C.	201092,	"	Sweeney, B.
200851,	"	Watt, T.	29959,	"	Harrison, J.
24320,	"	Masterton, J.	201203,	"	Gardner, A.
201049,	"	Anderson, D.	203536,	"	Stewart, A.
201158,	L/C.	McShane, A.	201257,	"	Gordon, J.
200157,	Pte.	Evans, H.	201401,	"	Fraser, W.
201385,	"	Conn, J.	29563,	"	Simpson, D.

"B" COY.

201135,	C.S.M.	Jones, J.	203295,	Sergt.	Bryden, J.
200199,	L/Sergt.	Irvine, S.	201732,	Corpl.	Fricker, H.
203265,	Corpl.	McLauchlan, J.	200252,	L/C.	McKenna, F.
204078,	Pte.	Brown, G.	200301,	Pte.	Conlin, J.
200322,	"	Christie, W.J.	200771,	"	Devlin, J.
200774,	"	Devlin, A.	203411,	"	Dickson, W.
201256,	"	Donaldson, J.	203281,	"	Fitzpatrick, A.
203280,	"	Gardner, J.	37496,	"	Gardiner, J.
201221,	"	Green, A.	200456,	"	Gibson, J.C.
37492,	"	Goldberg, H.	55857,	"	Gordon, A.
201713,	"	Harrison, H.	204080,	"	Haxton, J.
200175,	"	Hutcheson, C.G.	55834,	"	Hendry, G.
55730,	"	Jackson, J.	201161,	"	Keenan, W.
200280,	"	Lowe, W.	200941,	"	Loan, J.
203283,	"	McKay, B.	55897,	"	McKenzie, J.
201152,	"	McPhee, E.	201405,	"	McGowan, A.
201551,	"	McAllister, J.	40736,	"	Robertson, J.L.
42288,	"	Sloan, T.C.	200320,	"	Stewart, J.
55795,	"	Shaw, D.	200786,	"	Smith, A.
201715?	"	Smith, D.	201697,	"	Scott, W.
200812,	"	Tait, W.	B21410,	"	Travis, J.
55876,	"	Wallace, C.	55867,	"	Warden, J.
41891,	"	Ward, H.	204070,	Sergt.	Sharp, A.
200664,	Sergt.	Dobbie, T.	A/9039,	L/C.	Wood, W.
200510,	L/C.	McIntyre, D.	27231,	"	Beresford, R.
201139,	Pte.	Barclay, J.	55734,	Pte.	Baillie, W.R.

55733,	Pte.	Brown, A.	29150,	Pte.	Barr, A.
200277,	"	Christie, G.W.	55305,	"	Copeland, C.
55736,	"	Campbell, A.	200756,	"	Docherty, C.
200336,	"	Dow, J.	203289,	"	Duncan, A.
201374,	"	Divers, W.	201559,	"	Fleming, H.
203291,	"	Follett, E.	204071,	"	Gemmill, R.
203286,	"	Gilliver, G.	25153,	"	Graham, W.
201588,	"	Glendinning, J.	55870,	"	Gray, A.S.
201516,	"	Grant, A.	204703,	"	Hutton, J.
39609,	"	Hammond, J.	200178,	"	Hutchison, W.
200022,	"	Jones, W.	201154,	"	Kennedy, A.
42165,	"	Lowe, S.	36865,	"	Learmont, R.K.
201364,	"	Monaghan, H.	200387,	"	Morrison, T.
204072,	"	McMichael, R.	55849,	"	McKenna, J.
201559,	"	McKenzie, S.	204076,	"	McGill, A.L.
201412,	"	McEwan, A.	201426,	"	McLean, G.
200569,	"	McKie, R.	201504,	"	McColl, J.
55737,	"	McLeish, J.	201417,	"	McMillan, H.
201652,	"	McMannus, F.	55847,	"	Norrie, J.
200780,	"	Nicol, J.	200898,	"	O'Donnell, A.
55861,	"	Ruddick, R?	200722,	"	Reid, G.H.
201056,	"	Stewart, J.	55741,	"	Tilsley, H.
50566,	"	Thomson, D.	200297,	"	Wyllie, J.F.
200443,	"	Murphy, D.	200384,	C.Q.M.S.	Graham, J.
200038,	Sergt.	Gibbon, C.	201972,	L/Sergt.	Marrs, J.
200488,	Corpl.	Campbell, P.	200154,	Corpl.	McKenney, R.
200429,	L/C.	Miller, R.G.	55807,	L/C.	Cooper, W.
201963,	"	Gray, G.	50155,	Pte.	Alford, J.
200187,	Pte.	Brown, J.	55853,	"	Booth, E.
200524,	"	Brown, J.	200536,	"	Baker, W.A.
36624,	"	Campbell, D.	55873,	"	Cunningham, W.
200537,	"	Chandler, H.F.	203300,	"	Craig, J.
201389,	"	Clark, W.	200428,	"	Duguid, A.
55761,	"	Dowie, H.R.	201647,	"	Dawson, G.
55767,	"	Dunn, B.	55766,	"	Evans, L.
201454,	"	Fowler, J.	200454,	"	Finlayson, J.
55783,	"	Gilbert, J.	55810,	"	Gilfeather, P.
200335,	"	Gray, J.	201379,	"	Goodwin, J.
203080,	"	Hamilton, T.	243028,	"	Kilpatrick, A.
201639,	"	Innes, J.	201093,	"	Lamb, J.
55891,	"	Law, G.	200824,	"	Marsh, J.
26601,	"	Main, J.	55896,	"	Monagle, S.
55835,	"	Murray, W.	201731,	"	Morrison, H.
202216,	"	McGahan, P.	55826,	"	McFarlane, D.
200531,	"	McKenzie, A.	281634,	"	McGowan, A.
201323,	"	Riley, J.	15171,	"	Robertson, S.
200518,	"	Sweeney, A.M.	50034,	"	Stewart, R.
200166,	"	Smith, D.	200153,	"	Sweeney, M.
55875,	"	Thomson, T.	203293,	"	Thomson, J.
55866,	"	Urquhart, A.	203267,	"	Webster, A.
200333,	"	Whyte, W.F.	200275,	Sergt.	McLaren, D.
200216,	Sergt.	Quinn, J.	201702,	Corpl.	Burton, A.
201718,	Corpl.	Sutcliffe, P.	201425,	L/C.	Henderson, W.
203091,	Pte.	Anderson, M.	55854,	Pte.	Allison, R.
41587,	"	Beattie, W.	30093,	"	Burt, A.
202149,	"	Boyce, P.J.	203517,	"	Buckley, R.
201099,	"	Bogin, P.	202415,	"	Condie, J.
203292,	"	Cornish, A.J.C.	201424,	"	Craigon, T.
55894,	"	Crawford, W.	201022,	"	Concannon, J.
201415,	"	Dickson, A.	201398,	"	Duff, J.
202176,	"	Fulton, M.	203420,	"	Guy, J.
27648,	"	Gavin, R.	55731,	"	Gunderson, W.
50560,	"	Horne, A.	201482,	"	Kirkwood, E.
204074,	"	Kirk, J.	36810,	"	Lang, T.R.
200696,	"	Lang, R.	55872,	"	Melvin, D.W.
201409,	"	Miller, J.	201433,	"	Morrison, D.
201457,	"	Melville, R.	203423,	"	McGibbon, J.
200994,	"	McCann, J.	34732,	"	McCleneghen, J.
200644,	"	McCann, G.	36525,	"	McMillan, A.

31746,	Pte.	McKenzie, K.	21935, Pte.	Price, H.
203635,	"	Provan, A.	203301, "	Row, G.
200328,	"	Reid, J.	55831, "	Robbie, A.
201550,	"	Robertson, A.	28826, "	Thomson, J.M.
201066,	"	Traynor, J.	201543, "	Watson, W.
55879,	"	Weir, J.	201496, "	Finlay, J.
202099,	"	McGregor, A.	203421, "	Smith, R.
200398,	"	Terrace, P.	29532, "	McPherson, J.

"C" COY.

200010,	C.S.M.	Coubrough, J.	200271, C.Q.M.S.	Leitch, R.
200193,	L/C.	Morrison, W.	200317, L/C.	Burns, J.
200498,	Pte.	Bennett, R.	200820, Pte.	Hamilton, J.
201724,	"	Browne, R.	200729, "	Kinnaird, G.
40404,	"	Wordie, W.	37484, "	Cohen, J.
36705,	"	Craig, R.	35636, "	Hodge, R.
200315,	"	Kilgour, P.	200072, "	Chester, J.
201725,	"	Devaney, C.	200351, "	Earle, W.
200167,	"	McCusker, V.	201589, "	Heggie, A.
201695,	"	McAllister, S.	282491, "	Allardyce, T.
200513,	"	Grant, G.	201984, "	Logan, J.
200834,	"	Gemmell, T.	200630, "	Johnston, H.
201063,	"	McDonald, A.	26739, "	McArdle, J.
202151,	"	Boyd, G.	200245, "	Hesse, K.
202199,	"	Stewart, T.	203430, "	McLeod, H.
200127,	Corpl.	Gemmell, J.	27235, Corpl.	Hamilton, W.
23649,	"	Simpson, J.	200405, L/C.	Duff, D.
201122,	L/C.	McIntosh, J.	203071, Pte.	Alexander, J.
200829,	Pte.	Bryne, L.	22384, "	Bowie, J.
35484,	"	Constable, R.	202153, "	Dick, W.
38947,	"	Findlater, G.	200719, "	Fraser, J.
2986,	"	Finlayson, W.	201480, "	Hemphill, G.
201105,	"	Howat, H.	281233, "	Hannah, A.
28627,	"	Johnstone, S.	201033, "	Laird, G.
39785,	"	Leggate, G.	200352, Sergt.	Goodwin, I.
30497,	"	Marshland, S.	201319, Pte.	Mitchell, W.
9315,	"	Mitchell, R.	200590, "	McCormack,
200358,	"	McLean, H.	42882, "	Nixon, L.
3962,	"	Paton, G.	30384, "	Pitt, W.
39789,	"	Ross, J.	50569, "	Sinclair, S.
203047,	"	Strachan, J.	203048, "	Speid, D.
201467,	"	Swanson, J.	201701, "	Tomanie, T.
50567,	"	Tulloch, T.	201015, "	Livey, A.
202156,	"	Devine, E.	201558, "	Ferguson, P.
201723,	"	Stone, J.	200310, L/C.	Stirling, W.
201964,	Sergt.	Chalder, D.	211420, Sergt.	Humphreys, G.H.
201205,	Corpl.	Bowers, P.	200278, Corpl.	Paterson, A.C.
200631,	L/C.	Parker, W.	243030, Pte.	Clark, A.
51054,	Pte.	Gray, W.	201141, "	Headridge, J.
31852,	"	McIntyre, H.	200751, "	McKenzie, D.
38227,	"	Russell, G.	36849, "	Smith, V.
203055,	"	Stevens, G.	203045, "	Austin, W.
28850,	"	Clason, G.	200783, "	McLean, G.
200062,	"	Phillips, G.S.	201590, "	Devlin, J.
200778,	"	Kearney, C.	200345, "	McPhillamy, A.
201587,	"	O'Rourke, P.	28706, "	Hunter, W.
201676,	"	Campbell, G.	36283, "	Buchanan, H.
38473,	"	King, G.	40812, "	Lewis, W.
201156,	"	McLellan, C.	203410, "	McFayden, G.
29061,	"	Smullen, G.	201522, "	Skivington, C.
200739,	"	Cowie, D.	9305, "	Johnstone, C.
201617,	"	Nolan, P.	200419, "	Raeside, F.
36982,	"	Davidson, J.	38994, "	Hopkinson, F.
32756,	"	Derbyshire, P.	246988, "	McEwan, W.
29985,	"	Dinney, E?	201621, "	McFarlane, A.
200608,	Corpl.	Hill, J.	23754, Sergt.	Stark, A.
203066,	Sergt.	Higgins, R.	200877, Corpl.	Davidson, J.
200358,	Corpl.	Rowley,	31128, L/C.	Maxwell, J.

-5-

39610,	Pte.	Buyers, J.		333942,	Pte.	Brown, R.
20217,	"	Coulter, T.		202202,	"	Coyle, J.
201076,	"	Campbell, J.		36276,	"	Gilmartin, J.
201645,	"	Gallacher, J.		200998,	"	Laurie, J.
21183,	"	Little, F.		9311,	"	Laing, A.
200561,	"	Milwain, G.		23987,	"	McMahon, J.
29838,	"	Morrison, R.		37040,	"	McFarlane, J.
40624,	"	Morrison, N.		40273,	"	Moffat, A.
202187,	"	McLauchlan, J.		203406,	"	McFarlane, D.
202174,	"	McDougall, A.		201434,	"	McKenna, J.
9188,	"	McKinlay, R.		9337,	"	Nicholson, A.
40305,	"	Pow, G.		20795,	"	Paterson, G.
201200,	"	Paton, A.		29566,	"	Skedd, A.
20352,	"	Stewart, N.		9520,	"	Wood, P.
200604,	"	Glass, J.		201182,	"	Stirling, J.
201505,	"	Haugh, E.		9343,	"	Ross, D.
40287,	"	McLaughlan, J.		200803,	"	Isherwood, J.
7651,	"	Nelson, J.		200875,	Corpl.	McGroarty, W.
200130,	Sergt.	Harold, R.		200352,	"	Monaghan, J.
200504,	Corpl.	Stevenson, M.		330081,	L/Sergt.	Brown,
201421,	L/C.	Little,		24683,	Pte.	Williamson,
35749,	Pte.	Mair,		55811,	"	James,
55787,	"	Sharp,		37473,	"	Lamond,
200548,	"	Henney, J.		50568,	"	Conroy,
36333,	"	Clark, P.		36307,	"	Worke,
50159,	"	Martin,		200242,	"	Dinning.
201517,	"	Johnstone,		330330,	"	Sutherland,
55827,	"	McArthur,		201038,	"	Sadler,
201332,	L/C.	McGuire,		200370,	"	Henney, W.
50556,	Pte.	Farrell,		55770,	"	Jones, W.
201321,	"	McKim,		200486,	"	Stokes,
50559,	"	Haley,		201608,	"	Borland,
54920,	"	Tolland,		201563,	"	Morrison,
42524,	"	Marshall,		35734,	"	Laurie,
201376,	"	Miller, R.		203650,	"	Peace,
40295,	"	Merry, J.		200642,	"	Devenport,
200870,	"	Stewart, R.		36340,	"	Mitchell, J.
29722,	"	Patrick, D.		21307,	"	Wylie, R.
201276,	"	Maloney, W.		201302		Urquhart, L.

"D" COY.

200099,	C.S.M.	Waddell, J.		200230,	C.Q.M.S.	Angus, J.
200400,	L/C.	Smillie, D.		200117,	Pte.	McCabe, F.
36337,	Pte.	Jamieson, A.		200963,	"	Paterson, R.
36821,	"	Dick, T.		201309,	"	Doleman, W.
201642,	"	Mulholland, C?		31990,	"	Clark, W.
32812,	"	Cavanagh, J.		28506,	"	Logan, A.
34042,	"	Black, J.		201735,	"	Russell, J.
200610,	"	Hamilton, G.		201630,	"	O'Connor, E.
203089,	"	Woodrow, H.M.		40940,	"	Mitchell, D.
200668,	"	Mullen, J.		200710,	"	Close, J.
201450,	"	Smith, J.		201670,	"	Gray, W.
201061,	"	Samson, W.		31020,	"	Buchanan, R.
201959,	"	Anderson, W.		200402,	"	Scullion, J.
330337,	"	Harley, J.		24807,	"	Giles, W.
203094,	"	Gordon, J.		201594,	"	Martin, J.
200860,	"	Docherty, R.		34477,	"	Williams, A.
201468,	"	Cameron, W.		200444,	"	McDonald, R.
200163,	Sergt.	Sutherland, W.C.		201027,	Sergt.	Watson, W.
200452,	Corpl.	McLean, J.P.		201593,	Corpl.	Beattie, R.
14065,	L/C.	Fletcher, R.		50107,	Pte.	Findlay, W.
42125,	Pte.	Mackay, F.		40776,	"	Cumming, T.
40890,	"	Mulheron, P.		41437,	"	Cruickshanks, R.
37549,	"	Carr, J.		36803,	"	Craig, W.
201734,	"	McCabe, A.		200943,	"	Lawrie, D.
37508,	"	Ingram, J.		28859,	"	Barrie, J.
28569,	"	Brown, G.		203725,	"	Glen, W.

40392,	Pte.	Murison, J.		21181,	Pte.	Graham, E.
25912,	"	Beggan, F.		203082,	"	Burns, M.
28893,	"	Bowers, W.		38304,	"	McGonigal, J.
43748,	"	Cooper, J.B.		201559,	"	Irvine, W.
201062,	L/C.	McNaught, R.S.		39673,	"	McDonald, W.
200065,	Pte.	Leggett, J.M.		201568,	"	Hunter, A.
200266,	Sergt.	Smith, D.		200708,	Corpl.	Miller, F.
200265,	Corpl.	Hamilton, J.		34032,	Pte.	Thomson, J.
201553,	Pte.	McKenzie, J.		200814,	"	Michael, M.
23762,	"	Moore, J.		39737,	"	Summers, A.
201447,	"	McDonald, G.		203959,	"	McCafferty, J.
36823,	"	McCann, J.		201460,	"	Simpson, W.
202213,	"	Quigg, J.		200544,	"	Lennox, A.
50557,	"	Connelly, T.		50563,	"	Orr, W.
201739,	"	Craig, P;		41161,	"	Swan, P.
35680,	"	Clark, D.G.		39724,	"	Walters, D.
38080,	"	Donald, W.		29845,	"	McCallum, L.
50152,	"	Jack, W.		26855,	"	Bruce, J.
201145,	"	Brand, G.		202105,	"	Stroyan, C.
200446,	"	McLean, J.G.		27212,	"	McQuillan, J.
203694,	"	Warrick, J.		30595,	"	Summers, J.
9215,	"	Revie, N.		34913,	"	Duncan, J.
26334,	"	Cockburn, J.		38077,	"	Russell, J.
203096,	"	McLeod, R.		203272,	L/C.	McMillan, R.
201738,	Pte.	McLean, J.		3/21063,	Sergt.	Shaw, C.
200067,	L/Sergt.	Gair, W.		200035,	Corpl.	Devine, W.
201719,	L/Corpl.	McEwing, J.		201730,	Pte.	Aughey, J.
29599,	Pte.	Bolson, E.		201192,	"	Brady, P.
40857,	"	Bryson, A.		202104,	"	Burnett, J.
42341,	"	Chitty, E.		200920,	"	Crawley, M.
1539,	"	Donnelly, J.		25917,	"	Kirk, W.
26464,	"	McGoldrick, J.		9457,	"	McIntyre, H.
12439,	"	McMahon, H.		200179,	"	Main, J.
38091,	"	Mitchell, J.		41667,	"	Murphy, J.
200550,	"	Munsil, R.		200355,	"	O'Neil, W.
201264,	"	Ramsay, J.		40323,	"	Stevenson, J.
200546,	"	Stewart, W.		201458,	"	Tierney, J.
19426,	"	Watson, R.		201729,	"	Webster, J.
201623,	"	Wilson, T.		203832,	"	Whitwam, R.
201637,	"	Shepherd, J.		9197,	"	Mill, T.
201245,	"	Dornan, W.		201626,	"	McLaughlin, D.
203078,	Corpl.	McCracken, R.		43000,	"	Morrison, D.
203074,	Pte.	Robertson, D.		40905,	"	Gunning, J.
200226,	"	Kelly, W.		200568,	"	Anderson, E.
200122,	"	Tighe, A.		200250,	Corpl.	Hogg, J.
203077,	L/Corpl.	Paterson, P.		200305,	Pte.	McKay, F.
201014,	Pte.	Ross, J.		200133,	"	Adams, A.
50562,	"	Monaghan, J.		203042,	"	Timney, P.
201939,	"	Stevenson, J.		201064,	"	Wood, D.
203730,	"	Pte Lees, W.		23106,	"	Irvine, S.
29139,	"	McGonigal, M.		201565,	"	Green, R.
38707,	"	Campbell, A.		203732,	"	Elrick, W.
50106,	"	Brome, F.		200892,	"	Mooney, N.
203279,	"	Stevenson, R.		201610,	"	Whitfield, W.
50096,	"	Mackie, W.		201320,	"	Watson, J.
20043,	"	Gill, N.		200482,	"	McCallum, J.
201440,	"	McGarrity, P.		201438,	"	McBain, R.
13233,	"	McKinnon, R.		50105,	"	Thomson, A.
200088,	Sergt.	Smith, P.		203087,	"	Jordan, P.
35976,	Pte.	Parker, W.		201606,	"	Robb, R.
200447,	Sergt.	Graham, J.S.		200070,	Sergt.	Armstrong, N.
200132,	L/Sergt.	Stoddart, J.		36559,	Corpl.	Birrell, G.
201595,	L/Corpl.	Bell, J.		203089,	Pte.	Mowat, H.
9077,	Pte.	Auld, N.		9088,	"	Bowman, G.
27221,	"	Murray, H.		38989,	"	Duncan, L.
38214,	"	Bruin, G.		9320,	"	Malloy, W.
200123,	"	Adam, J.		4520,	"	Kyle, D.
201600,	"	Stewart, T.		200092,	"	Adams, J.

201386,	Pte.	Simpson, W.	20964,	Pte.	Campbell, T.
200439,	"	Allardice, M.	201452,	"	Walker, J.
201671,	"	Boyle, J.	916,	"	Hagan, C.
200098,	"	Hamilton, M.	29669,	"	Paterson, D.
200489,	"	Glen, A.	944,	"	Hannigan, W.
200162,	"	Marshall, J.	200329,	"	Rule, G.
201369,	"	Armstrong, J.	200685,	"	Sloan, A.
4818,	"	Laidlaw, W.	50542,	"	Barclay, A.
36165,	"	Moffat, W.	17751,	"	Bellew, J.
33859,	"	Coleman, P.			

TRANSPORT SECTION.

200016,	Sergt.	Birrell, R.	200689,	Corpl.	Masterton, H.
200097,	Corpl.	Small, W.	200030,	L/Corpl.	McLeod, H.
200262,	L/Corpl.	Birrell, T.H.	200543,	"	Harvey, D.
201275,	Pte.	Brawley, W.	200602,	Pte.	Lowrie, M.
200999,	"	McGhee, P.	200923,	"	Shearer, R.
203059,	"	Smith, M.	201178	"	Turner, W.
201451,	"	Bruce, K.	201422,	"	O'Rourke, A.
200647,	"	Cooke, W.	201075,	"	Brodie, A.
200332,	"	Hawkins, C.	200408,	"	Smith, J.
215329,	"	McDonald, E.	200545,	"	Kerr, S.H.
203277,	"	Mulholland, H.	201711,	"	Reilly, W.
38835,	"	McGinn, M.	200626,	"	McRae, J.
31654,	"	Russell, J.	9176,	"	McBride, W.
201195,	"	Turnbull, R.	201552,	"	Allison, J.
201111,	"	McCrimmon, A.	201520,	"	Church, J.
200789,	"	Curran, J.	201050,	"	Farrell, J.
201418,	"	Gallacher, J.	201136,	"	Greening, J.
203085,	"	Houston, R.	201139,	"	Connelly, J.
201612,	"	Park, A.	203403,	"	McDonald, D.
200082,	"	Sweeney, H.	214551,	"	Anderson, J.
200768,	"	Scott, J.	200537,	"	Salmon, J.
200980,	"	Kelly, J.	201195,	"	Kerr, J.
200063,	"	Menzies, J.	201633,	"	Flynn, H.
200766,	"	Smith, G.	50556,	"	Grimley, W.
200256,	"	Cranston, J.	201125,	"	Kilpatrick, T.
203419,	"	Mann, A.	201043,	"	McBrayne, R.
200309,	"	Raeside, J.	203072,	"	Robertson, A.
201477,	"	Whitehill, J.	201149,	"	Penman, J.
201444,	"	Spence, J.	T4/091792,	"	McBeath, C.
201371,	"	Darroch, H.	T4/246996,	"	Johnstone, H.
17235,	"	Allan, W.	31842,	"	Graham, J.
42265,	"	Paton, R.	27165,	"	Mulhill, T.
203405,	"	Purdin, W.	200197,	"	Banford, R.
211453,	"	McMenamin,	50151,	"	McMahon, H.
203516,	"	Walker, J.	201197,	"	Gow, A.
33341,	"	Gordon, J.	201638,	"	McNamara,
201077,	"	Beattie, W.	201662,	"	Dowdells, J.
200858,	"	Scott, J.	201264,	"	Slessor, A.
200043,	"	Wilson, D.	201150,	"	Hamilton,
201306,	"	Forbes, J.	9128,	"	Dickson, J.
201669,	"	Semple, J.	9405,	"	Donaldson, H.
200627	"	Meechan, J.			

HEADQUARTERS COY.

200451,	Sergt.	Nolan, J.	200528,	Corpl.	Kelly, E.
200684,	L/Corpl.	Burke, R.	2898,	L/Corpl.	Birrell, R.
202101,	Pte.	Littlejohn, D.	200029,	Pte.	Burns, J.
9335,	"	Conway Connelly, P.	200532,	"	Brown, M.
55735,	"	Henderson, W.	204069,	"	Oliver, W.
55816,	"	Davidson, R.	55832,	"	Dawson, R.
55746,	"	McKelvie, W.	201564,	"	Mathieson, J.
200276,	"	Pirie, D.	200844,	"	Drummond, J.
200896,	"	Kinnieburgh, J.	200549,	"	McFarlane, G.
203068,	"	Johnstone, A.	40430,	"	Smith, W.
29858,	"	Peacock, J.	19278,	"	Robertson, G.

19260,	Pte.	Ward, J.		19422,	Pte.	Rae, J.B.
200066,	"	Ross, S.		200537,	"	Nixon, E.
201666,	"	Wylie, J.		200300,	Sergt.	Ashmore, R.
200184,	Sergt.	Taylor, T.		200169,	Corpl.	Palmer, J.
200414,	Pte.	Hamilton, D.		200174,	Pte.	Brisbane, D.
33173,	"	Mackie, E.		27834,	"	McMurray, H.
200399,	"	Cameron, R.		200061,	"	Nicol, W.
200307,	"	Clark, G.		200073,	"	Morgan, G.
200723,	"	Green, G.		200459,	"	Nixon, A.
36643,	"	Morrow, J.		200096,	"	Wright, W.B.
201571,	Sergt.	Arthur, A.		200179,	Piper	Reid, R.
12226,	Piper	Kennedy, C.		201330,	"	Clelland, T.
202169,	"	Connelly, J.		203664,	"	Thomson, A.
200143,	Drummer	Cubbage, W.		291960,	Drummer	Cockburn, J.
201187,	"	McGrory, J.		203081,	"	Young, A.
200683,	Sergt.	Paterson, A.		200275,	Pte.	Robertson, J.
200273,	Pte.	Kyle, A.		200131,	"	Hyland, W.
200715,	"	Niven, T.		200918,	"	Boyle, W.
201244,	"	Menzies, J.		201650,	"	Bell, R.
31684,	"	Todd, W.		200280,	"	McMurray, A.
200495,	Corpl.	McKerrow, A.		200681,	"	Hamil, E.
200221,	Pte.	Milne, J.		201084,	"	McGeachy, D.
200574,	"	Brown, F.		201172,	"	Riddell, G.
38200,	"	Russell, W.H.		200462,	R.Q.M.S.	Jennison, G.
200231,	Corpl.	Wilson, J.		201025,	L/Corpl.	Home, W.
200831,	Pte.	Morrison, D.		200607,	Pte.	Knight, T.
200516,	"	Hutcheon, R.		23276,	"	Dickson, P.
201430,	"	Bolesworth, T.		200437,	"	Munn, R.
200415,	Corpl.	McGarrity, G.		200329,	L/Corpl.	Bulloch, R.
200337,	Pte.	Park, R.		200811,	Pte.	Kane, C.
200832,	"	Craig, D.		201603,	"	McGhie, H.
200916,	"	McPherson, A.		200430,	Corpl.	Lennox, G.
200650,	"	Taylor, J.G.		200461,	Pte.	Kennedy, S.
200395,	"	Burnside, A.		200821,	"	Glancy, C.
201513,	"	Cassels, H.		200121,	"	Hutchison, R.
200706,	"	Gloag, D.		26879,	"	Murdoch,
200773,	"	Kirk, M.		201549,	"	Lewis, W.H.
200777,	Sergt.	Martin, T. A.O.C.		2838,	L/Sergt.	Palmer, V.
200600,	L/Corpl.	Glasgow, J.		200292,	Pte.	Fraser, J.
201252,	Pte.	Thomson, W.		201010,	"	Crichton, J.
201641,	"	Carswell, R.		33354,	"	McKay,
36493,	"	Williams, F.		201723,	"	Walker, W.
200015,	Sergt.	Lyon, R.		200553,	L/Corpl.	Ross, A.
200413,	Pte.	Smith, J.B.		200244,	R.S.M.	McKean, M.
201663,	"	Glass, M.		200201,	Sergt.	Cameron, F.C.
200152,	L/Corpl.	Sadler, R.		31644,	Pte.	Hamilton, R.
200992,	Sergt.	McNaught, J.		200474,	Sergt.	Meiklejohn, G.
200026,	"	Orr, D.		201740,	Pte.	McIntyre, J.P.
200758,	Pte.	McPhail, J.		200186,	L/Corpl.	McElwee, W.

1/5th H.L.I.

WAR DIARY

May 1918

Vol. XXXVI

36/1

Army Form C. 2118.

WAR DIARY
or
INTELLIGENCE SUMMARY: 5th H.L.I.
(Erase heading not required.)

Instructions regarding War Diaries and Intelligence Summaries are contained in F.S. Regs., Part II. and the Staff Manual respectively. Title pages will be prepared in manuscript.

Place	Date	Hour	Summary of Events and Information	Remarks and references to Appendices
LA LACQUE	1/5/18		Took O.C. Coys to 3rd line of defence & allotted Gr. frontages. Brigadier inspected transport in the afternoon. Capt M.G. CLARKE & 2.Coys/To. went to upper Bde. Reserve Coy. attached to 4/8th Coy. R.S. Day dull but fine.	
	2/5/18		Coys training foll. Special Rapport Spotting instructor gave one hours instruction to every platoon. Lt Col CAMPBELL GORDON HIGHLANDERS lectured to the Batt. on the use of the bayonet, inspected Nets - Found camp clean. Evening of men V.foor. arranged programme of musketry for 3/5 -	
	3/5/18		Coy foot & arms drill. Day cold & windy. Arranged programme of musketry training on ranges near WIRE, owing to all Coys except C. carried out short programmes of musketry training on ranges near WIRE, owing to no firing re. being on the ranges no men could not have individual firing. Some fired 5 rounds application & 10 rounds rapid at 200 yards range; S.O.R.1. being open. All L Gunners fired 120 rounds, some of which was fired evening S.A.A.. 18 officers attended the C-in-C advanced M.G. officers school. B. active in R.I.F.E. on the recent fighting. Day fine & warm foll.	
	4/5/18		Bde. less 5th A.M.E. marched at 07.30 to MAATES (G.33) to x 14th Corps reinforcement Camp to sub demonstration of cloud gas, Flammenwerfer, firegrenades, afternoon Bde marched to Some garrison on G.35 C.3.5. 9th Huxley held Batt. went through Gas chamber & returned independently to camp arriving at 08.15. Received warning order to move to XVIII Corps area. Sent Lt CLEMMING (Scout officer) R.O.M.S.; 1 Sergts & 3 no N.C.O. to see bus T.C. which Batt. was to take over. 6 H.C.O. & 34 men left for a 7 days musketry course at MATRINGHEM. Day hot & heavy S.A.M. foll.	
	5/5/18		Morning met Church Parade cancelled. Brought Bde. by route march for inspection. attended conference of Bde H.qs at 17.00. Batt. less 4 more and 6th aust. & team from A.I.E. to MARDEUIL - from here by road to NEUVILLE ST VAAST. also received to take over our	MANOSSA [?] 12.0[?]

WAR DIARY
INTELLIGENCE SUMMARY
(Erase heading not required.)

S.A.A.L.I

Army Form C. 2118.

34/2.

Instructions regarding War Diaries and Intelligence Summaries are contained in F.S. Regs., Part II. and the Staff Manual respectively. Title pages will be prepared in manuscript.

Place	Date	Hour	Summary of Events and Information	Remarks and references to Appendices
LA ACQUE	5/5/18		On night of 5th from 34th Batt. CANADIAN Infantry. Held conference with CO Coys & arranged details of move. Fell.	Appendices 1/20,000
	6/5/18.		Marched out of Camp at 0130. Entrained at AIRE at 1015 and arrived at MAROEUIL about 1600. Marched to huts at NEUVILLE ST VAAST arriving about 1900. Fell.	
NEUVILLE ST VAAST.	7/5/18.		Went with PC Coys, MO, O/C Sigs & 24 to VIMY. Items Pat. 34th Canadian Infantry had only 2 Coys in VIMY & they are required for working parties. Arranged relief of these 2 Coys & reconnoitred to BROWN LINE allotted to us thus: L.E. from GRAND TRUNK TRENCH on 7.26 a.3.8 to CYRIL TRENCH on S.11.a.1.8. Allotted two Coys, Batt H.Qrs, two trench mortars, two subaltern's staff & all officers Scouts to 20 + NCO trench Scouts in 13.Co.D. Nucleus. Hqrs administrative staff & all officers Scouts to 20 + NCO trench Scouts 19.13.C.D. Ready us per fire Section. B/f NEUVILLE ST VAAST at 1930 & arrived at VIMY at 2200. Relief complete 0130.	
VIMY.	8/5/18		Went round lines which were held as follows:- A.Coy from 7.26 a.3.8 to where BROWN LINE crosses the Rly. embankment at 7.20 C.0.9. C Coy from the Rly embankment (on N) S.24 d.5.8 to H.13. C by R.E. who were under my orders for tactical purposes from S.24 D.5.8 across the ARRAS RD to S.23 b.8.1. D. Coy from S.23 b.8.1 to CYRIC TRENCH on S.11 a.1.8. a total frontage of 1800 yards. Bttn H.Qs HILLBURY on Battle Reserve in VIMY. Platoon R.Coy Supplies Nucleus garrison for HILLSIDE. Here too long to hold continuously so conducted with keeping all scouts & warned by P.W. had energy might attack during night of 8/9/8. Night quiet, all quiet. Fell.	
	9/5/18.		Went round lines of A + C Coys and C.O. 113th Scottish Bn & arranged what work should be commenced. Saw O/Cs of 113th & Coys & discussed their dispositions at relief of Tuesday & Wednesday. Had conference with Company Commanders on the offensive & warned them that enemy attack was expected that night with a short bombardment commencing 2230. Night quiet.	

WAR DIARY
or
INTELLIGENCE SUMMARY.

Army Form C. 2118.

5 M.H.L.I. 39/8

Place	Date	Hour	Summary of Events and Information	Remarks and references to Appendices
VIMY	10/5/18		Lt. T. Hodson replaced 2/Lt. Pennon with Pannin Coy. Went over line and made following alterations in dispositions. Moy. to take from Rly to Lentenant (72 + 39) to 72.5 C 2.9. C by from 72.9 C 2.9 to Angres Rd (Cu) S 24 A S P. Sepler Coy mts 2 Hqu from Section of Scouts pushed forward. Forward is a Lewis Gun patrol noted Lens. Ackers Rd at S18 6.2.2. Right platoon of D Coy approves and same started out the L/Sg/t Mahone bought men to the right from S 17 d 38 to S 17 d 17. B Coy has 1 Platoon in Vimy no reserve. 1 Platoon Rly as reserve garrison of Hillside S 29 B Supp. G.C.O'Dwin wounded when on Bdy water guard. Night guard - 1/3 other ranks carried out Mericourt Road near Rly. 2 men very slightly gassed. Leave gum 4 Oph 1 each day + 1 officer every 14 days fell.	MARCOEUIL 1/20000
	11/5/18		Capt W. S. guard presented for men coln Hqu on Vimy. Selected armed gun emplacement at 72.5 a 6.2. Went round Vimy defences with OC 7 HLL1. Information received that batten would relieve 5 MHLI our Blue line on night 13/14. Night guard fell	
	12/5/18		Went with C Coys + O.Z.T. Scouts to Blue line + arranged details of relief with OC 7 HLL1 night guard fell. Received word that food lure was A.T. repacking out O.E.C. Troops 97, 5 HLL1. Party proportional whilst night on objete or 15th old was relieving 15th. On night of 13/14 + to keep one half of the their officers + Lst by 7, 5 HLL1. Return check worse at 3:00. Lt W.H. Milne wounded. Houne leave. Tomney shelled factory pastures in Gu. Caen Vimy. Ph Hobkinson C Coy killed by shelling. 1 gr. B Coy wounded. Day fine + clean from	Additions W P. I
	13/5/18		Night guard. Morning fine Bde sighted. News Drung most of the day. Most instructions have the old that the reorganization of the Red + Brown lines on to 200 years around night 13/14. Nova organization. Right Bath to hold area Vimy-Nova Scotia - Left Batn. Hotel Area. La Chaudière. White in reserve. Mid D Coy + 1 Platoon B Coy at Hillside must be relieved by 9/7 Batn. (5 MSH) That in relief Hd 6 A H.L.1 in Canada + 8 Platoon Kp C 3.4.5 OC 5 MSH arrived + details of relief of D Coy + 1 Platoon with Teddie Gerrard about T/Lt C 3.4 5 by 5 MSH to take over Known hill from TOC 5 Coys was ary B Coy arranged	

WAR DIARY
INTELLIGENCE SUMMARY

Army Form C. 2118.

35/W. 5/N.H.L.1.

Place	Date	Hour	Summary of Events and Information	Remarks and references to Appendices
VIMY	13/5/18		Orders to relieve the 1/4 Cys 6 N.H.I. on Canada Trench. Relief complete A Cy by 2030, B Cy by 2000, D Cy by 2030. 18 Other Ranks 1/20,000	WAR-CAL 6
		Cy 1130	Had conference with O.C. Cys at 1800 & discussed details of relief of 7 N.H.L.1 & made the necessary alterations in programme to Suit new disposition of Cys. Night quiet. Hill.	
	14/5/18		Went up to Blue Line & mount fort held by 7 N.H.L.1. Had final conference with O.C. Cys at 1800 & arranged times at which Cys were to move out. Batt. started to move 2100. Order of move A, D, B C Hqrs. Relief complete 0150. 3 O.R's B Cy wounded while proceeding over Ry embankment 7 N.H.I. carried out raid on enemy's front line at 713 C 07.40. No enemy were seen – no identification obtained. Boys BRAVO Went on home leave. Hill.	
	15/5/18		Misspent whole Raid, fairly during stand to & faulty in afternoon. noticed slackness in trench discipline. Had conference with O.C. Cys & discussed such situations. Day fact, quiet. 2 O.R's A Cy wounded by Shrapnel from A.A. Guns. Arranged for 2 battle patrols. Sound Sanitary arrangements very bad, instructed fire wood to make fly-proof seals. Depositeries of Cys. B from ACHEVILLE R.W. to La in BRUNSWICK. C Cy from B in BRUNSWICK to TOAST C.T. (ex). D Cy from TOAST (ex) to Quebec TOMMY C.T.(ex). A Cy from Tommy (ex) to VERTH TILLEY (ex). Capt A.D. CURRIE to Hospital. Capt MILLER took over command of B Cy. 2 battle patrols. Tht COTTEREL & 1 Platoon C Cy, & Th HARDIE & 1 Platoon A Cy. Neither reached their objective. Night quiet. 2 short bursts of gas-shelling – mainly Blue Cross. 1910 A Cy Frost & 1 O.R. wounded by Shell-fire. Hill.	
	16/5/18		Went round line, went to Batt. O.P. then up scheme for redistribution of Cys so as to give a Batt. Reserve. C.S.M. HANCOCK went on Leave, Liebius Athers Scouts & Officers, 1 Battle Patrol Lt. CANNING & 1 Platoon B Cy. Nothing of Enemy Seen.	
	17/5/18		Fine day. O.C. discussed fresh organization & redistribution of Cys on the Line. Informed that the Batto was to have 32 Rifle Sections & 16 Rifle Sections & 16 Grenade Sections. Cys looked new frontages – B Cy shown on tape. C Cy to move men lure Sents "the home front" from trenches of QUEBEC & UPSETT & TOAST C.T. (ex) with 2 Sections on "the left "in TOAST Coln NEW BRUNSWICK. D Cy on line from 70 NIST C.T (ex) to	

WAR DIARY or INTELLIGENCE SUMMARY

Army Form C. 2118.

3rd M.R.1

Place	Date	Hour	Summary of Events and Information	Remarks and references to Appendices
VIMY	17/5/18		TOMMY (inc) MAIN Louis Scouts 2 Platoons B Cy. 1st Class from TOMMY (inc) to VESTA TILLEY - MAIN Sunk M.M.20.54.46 Section Bulled in TOMMY. TOMMY (inc) to VESTA TILLEY (inc). HqCoy(inc) 2 Platoons in Bn Reserve. 1 Platoon a function of TOMMY TZ.QOTO & TOMST. 1 Platoon in TOMST above McDERMID C.T. Enemy shelled BATTERIES R4 & QUEBEC during afternoon & heavily shelled sain areas during the night. Rifles damaged & 2 guns emplacement blown in. Lt MACKENZIE M.O. to Hospital. Lt PARR had on terns leave. Pte HEMMING	
	18/5/18		& 1 Platoon D Coy on battle patrol - noticed of enemy. Lt MORTON from 2nd C.I.A arrived in place of H.O. Withdrew Platoons in the morning- prepared scheme for rehearsal. Day fair & warm. night good except for some shelling of our front line. Both Patrols Lt CARMICHAEL with 2nd Lt TODD H.Coy went to SASL's & Platoon B Coy. out to reconnoitre enemy wire T.1 B 6.0. Patrol got through outer wire - saw no trace of enemy front & rifle grenades into enemy main line fell.	
	19/5/18		Day fair & warm. 2 offs wounded by shellfire & 2 offs by knotty gun accident. Arranged details for relief by 7th A.H.R.I on night 20/21 Prepared defence scheme. Lt MORTON 2nd C.I.A relieved by Capt. STANSFIELD M.C. 3rd L.F.A. Battle patrol Sgt TURNER & 1 Platoon A Coy. took up defensive position about T.16 C.5.5. but saw no trace of the enemy Att.	
	20/5/18		Fine day & warm. Day quiet. The Cafe Commander H'quel Sec. 1 VOR MARSE Corner received tunic & exposed himself as pleased with what he saw. Relieved by 7th A.H.R.I relief completed 0200. Batt' occupied Vimy night SCOTIA Area. C Coy in CANADA TRENCH from NEW BRUNSWICK ROAD (inc) to MERICOURT Relief. H.Coy from MERICOURT RD (inc) to JULIA JAMES C.T. inc. B Coy in CROWN Hire from Rly embankment at T.26 a 39 to AVION ROAD (inc) & 2 Platoons D Coy from AVION RD (inc) to ANGRES RD (inc) D Coy (less 2 platoons) 2 Reserve in VIMY. Hqrs at T.27.a 9.8.-8.	

A1092/1. Wt. W12839/M1298. 750,000. 11/17. D. D. & L., Ltd. Forms/C2118/14.

WAR DIARY or INTELLIGENCE SUMMARY

Army Form C. 2118.

30/6.

5th H.Z. 1

(Erase heading not required.)

Place	Date	Hour	Summary of Events and Information	Remarks and references to Appendices
V.M.S.	22/5/18		night quiet. 18th	WAR DIARY
	23/5/18		Sunday. Splendid day. Went round lines & observed defensive posts of Coys. Mines arranged & 26000 fire not v. dry conditions within in rest. Received letter of appreciation from C.O. on work done on part of 1st Commonwealth R.S.C & 2/Lt TODD of C pointing out gallant action on patrol. Total casualties for tour of duty in front line 16. O.R.s killed 4 wounded 12.	
	24/5/18		Cold splendid weather. Col WATSON Vy Commander of 5th N.O.S.B. arrived to arrange reliefs. Made preliminary arrangements. Enemy shelled heavy battery near Hope Farm during day at 22.30/23.00 HYS & CONDA Trench heavily shelled with Gas & H.E. 2 killed 4 & wounded. CONDA HILL	
	25/5/18		Fine. Went round WILLERVAL Sectr. Quiet. AM	
	26/5/18		Rel'd by 5th N.O.S.B. Relief complete 11 at St BATT taken m buses to MT ST ELOI arriving about 02.30. Found by details & Transport HQ	
Mt ST ELOI	26/5/18		Day fine. All ranks resting. New clothing issued to B.C & D Coys. Went round Barracks in afternoon. Heads in low position. Conference of Coy officers at BHQ at 14.00 discussed training. Capt GIROT to Hospital Sick.	
	27/5/18		At NORTH FARN Lt MCINNES reported. Officers Camp much cleaner situated. Day fine. Church Parade 0930 Rev MSINNES. G.O.C. Division came round in afternoon & inspected huts. Chief grievance XVIII corps expected movements & agreed hereby material for improvement & also toilets &c AM. Enemy shelled camp with H.V. guns direct hit on hut occupied by 2nd L.F.A. 12 killed 13 wounded training begun alloc's RSM breakfast. Enemy continued in morning & again still training in afternoon. Day fine. AM	

WAR DIARY
or
INTELLIGENCE SUMMARY.

Army Form C. 2118.

5⁄ H.L.I.   36/7

Place	Date	Hour	Summary of Events and Information	Remarks and references to Appendices
MT ST ELOY	28/5/18		Day fine. Coys training in rib trys on the Bermuil Course. Lt M. H. MICHIE returned from U.K. leave. 2/Lt PENMAN went to 1 S.H.B. HQ	WAR DIARY 1/5 5500
	29/5/18		Day fine. All Coys training. Day fine & fairbien on open range. Bath Supr Sergt Worsley went from B+C that afternoon in motor lorries to the ECOIVRES & training a detachment. Batt. confined to camp in consequence of period in not felt	
	30/5/18		Forty four. All training stopped. men engaged digging trench manned Neds interests men from Skill Fire. Day fine & warm fall	
	31/5/18		Day fine & warm. All Coys still engaged digging on the back Bremey Shallow Council with H.V. Guns. No Casualties. Received orders for relief of 4 D.S. on Right sub-section of Right Section of Divisional Sector during daylight on 2nd June.	
			Total Casualties in May.	
			Killed O/Rs 3	
			Wounded " 29	
			Died of Wounds O/Rs 1 27 ORs	
			To Hospital Sick Officers 2 O/Rs 124	
			Rejoined from hospital O/Rs 40	
			" " 72	

JB Wilson Lt Col
Commanding 1/5 H.L.I.

Vol 3

9 G.
16 sheets

5th H. L. I.

WAR DIARY

June 1918

Vol 37

WAR DIARY or INTELLIGENCE SUMMARY

Army Form C. 2118.

27/1 S.W.H.2. 1

Place	Date	Hour	Summary of Events and Information	Remarks and references to Appendices
MT ST ELOY	16/1/18		Went to WILLERVAL. Hqrs of Royal Scots and arranged details of relief. Went round line with Lt Col MITCHELL. Had conversation with Lt. Bay-four weather very cold, raining snow & [?] snow. Wheeled put fuel on Open range before front & trenches. Sketches fair - guns still new. 2/Lt NICOLSON goes to B.Co on successful signalling Officer Pill.	Appendix 1 20.059
WILLERVAL	2/2/18		Relieved 11th Royal Scots in Right Subsector of Right Section of Divisional Sector. Brussels TRENCH. Move began at 11.00 relief completed 17.30. Day fine. Capt H SCOTT-BROWN Battnqrbtal. Night quiet. Pill.	Appendix No 2
	3/2/18		Had conference with Co Commander with regard to reorganisation of Coys. Went round line with O.C. A Coy fine. Quiet night quiet. Pill. 2/Lt LEE MRE goes on Patrol. Leave. Pill.	
	4/2/18		B.J.C. again in the line with regard to proposed reorganization. 2/Lt Sanderson, 2/Lt SAUNDERSON & 2/Lt Robertson Patrols out. South of O Sector. Capt MILLER D Coy killed accidentally when returning from patrol by shot fired by sentry in his trench. Night quiet. Pill.	
	5/2/18		Day fine. 2/Lt GIBBONS, 2/Lt LEY & 1 other Rank. Lt MALCOLM & KILSBY 90% 5 weeks Platoon Commanders Course. Lt J.H. PARK returns from Home leave. Relieve 2nd S.HIGHLDN B.Co. 2/Lt TURNER Ply. tested S.O.S. to artillery barrage. Could not get Artillery to answer own Call by wire. Night quiet Pill.	
	6/2/18		Day fine wilderness. Wounded by rifle by 7/R.H.L. on 05. Capt R B CURRIE from hospital. Day quiet. Patrols 2/Lt COTTERELL C.Coy. W PARK D.Coy. Night quiet Pill.	
	7/2/18		Day fine. O.C. 7th H.L.I. came up & arranged details of relief. Day quiet. Warned that during night attack. All Coys wearing men round line. Patrols laid down to minimum. Night quiet Pill.	
	8/2/18		Relieved by 7/H.L.I. Batt: then becoming Right Reserve Battn of right Section of divisional sector.	Appendix 12 No 2

Army Form C. 2118.

WAR DIARY
or
INTELLIGENCE SUMMARY.

(Erase heading not required.)

37/2   5th H.L.I.

Place	Date	Hour	Summary of Events and Information	Remarks and references to Appendices
WILLERVAL	8/4/18		Relief completed noon except for 3 platoons of B Coy which were relieved after dark. Handed over to Major CRAWFORD & went to RISSIN CAMP for 6 days rest. PAH	Map 36NWB S9. 1: 1/20 000
	9/4/18		Inspected Incomplete or fighting order — great improvement since last inspection. Men tech out agains wind during show of chaff. Rifle exam: Inspection changed as follows — BROWN LINE from WESTERN Rd to TIRED ALLEY inclusive was held by 2 Coys with frontage & platoon in BROWN LINE with 2 platoons in Reserve. Coy at B867. behind Ry embankment — C Coy battalion from TIRED ALLEY inclusive to FAMBUS WILLERVA & Rd (exc.) - B Coy from WILLERVAL Rd (inc) to WESTERN Rd (inc) - C Coy forming 2 Reserve posts with 2 of Brigade on TIRED ALLEY at S9 C 2.3 & B.13 d.2.2. HQrs. in SPIN, FAMBUS, TATE & BORDER Post. D Coy Reserve. Work done on dugging emplacements for Lewis Liftpads & wiring. Ray front fell	
	10/4/18		Major CRAWFORD inspected BROWN LINE. Sundries as placed on tod sanitation, no dug outs or shelters. Coys worked on making emplacements & on wire. B Coy took over Water & Rations parties from D Coy. Head Vertically from Ash Noel Baton invalid to possibly called on to do a daylight raid. Supported on ROEUX. D Coy detailed to carry out raid. Senr Officers reconnoitred TIRED ALLEY with a view to using same in the raid. Inspected Band & Buglers. Protested dental party fell	
	11/4/18		Major CRAWFORD reconnoitred front line with regard to raid. OC D Coy with Platoon Commanders & Sergeant also covered all recce.nnaissance. FAMBUS POST shelled throughout day. No Casualties. Inspected Nucleus at GIRVAN to leave fell.	
	12/4/18		Went to WILLERVAL and arranged for relief by JJ H.L.I. on 14th. Major CRAWFORD visited B. C & D Coys. Day fine. MORRISON DUMP heavily shelled fell.	
	13/4/18		Inspected Incomplete Equipment. Weather still fine. Visited Reserve bath on TIRED ALLEY. Coy commander proceeded to 7th H.L.I. to arrange relief. fell	

WAR DIARY or INTELLIGENCE SUMMARY

Army Form C. 2118.

5th H.L.I.

Place	Date	Hour	Summary of Events and Information	Remarks and references to Appendices
WILLERVAL	14/4/18		Took over Front Line from 7 K.H.L.I. A.B.Y.C. Coys. Blue Zone, D. Coy. Posts. Relief complete 18.10. Major CRAWFORD gone to K.O.S.B. A command and Lecturing return of Lt.Col. COULSON from leave. NONE + OTTAWA much heavily shelled at 21.00. 200 S.O.S. sent from C Coy at 24.00. Reinforced 2.8. 2000 men C. Coy proceeded Posts.	Appendices No. 1, 2, 3
	15/4/18		Day fine - westerly wind. Patrols Lt. CUMMING with Hqs. scouts 4th BRODIE with 2 Section C. Coy. Night quiet. 2/Lt. DILLINGHAM + 4 N.C.O.s B. Coy. S.M. SIMMONS attached for instructions in Scouting & Intelligence work.	
	16/4/18		Day fine & quiet. Would Motherly 10-00 night to bombard & shoot patrols would have to follow up bombardment to see what damage had been done to enemy wire. 2/Lt. TURNER with patrol of 3 ORs went to enemy wire - saw wire + own Posts in WILLERVAL - MALLEY x of. Had to withdraw. Coys. working. 1 OR wounded A.Coy.	
	17/4/18		Fine morning - showery afternoon evening. Received orders that C.R.C.A. would relieve Batt. on 20th night. Very quiet. The ORKNEYS with 2 Section B. Coy. reconnoitred enemy wire in MALLEY + LOOP. WIRE. Found wire badly damaged. Patrol.	
	18/4/18		Day fine. Arranged details of relief on 20.4. wiring scheme for following of bombardment of salient on enemy side of wire. 2 ORs + 1 NCO wounded. Pocketten patrol passed from C. Coy. B. Coy S. wiring - Patrol.	
	19/4/18		Day showery. Received orders that C.C. Coys. also programme of wiring which in reserve. 2/Lt. LEGATE from M.G. base. Patrol.	
	20/4/18		Relieved by 5.R.S.F. Relief complete 19.00. Coys marched independently to HUTS CAMP NEWVILLE ST.VAAST. Day Showery. Go M.L. with Capt. GRAFTON inspected for duty. Patrol.	Appendices No. 6.
	21/4/18		Next arrival Camp. Day fine but cloudy. Appointed Lt. HAMILTON Capt. + Lt. DRUMMOND & Sergt. HIGGINS M.C. Alltype cleaning + ablution. Inspected draft of 13 ORs. which included Master Cook, Bell.	
	22/4/18		A.B.C. Coys at musketry. Very windy. G.O.C. Division inspected Camp. P.R.A.O. took out in Orderly Rm. Bell.	

Army Form C. 2118.

Instructions regarding War Diaries and Intelligence Summaries are contained in F.S. Regs., Part II. and the Staff Manual respectively. Title pages will be prepared in manuscript.

WAR DIARY or INTELLIGENCE SUMMARY.

(Erase heading not required.)

3. 1. H. L. I.

Place	Date	Hour	Summary of Events and Information	Remarks and references to Appendices
NEUVILLE ST VAAST	23/6/18		Inspected HANSON CAMP as a possible place for 2 Coys as H.Q. LT. CAMP unoccupied. Found strong smell. Bde Conference at 1630. New programme of training necessary as all training not done between 0900 & 1200. Rest no unus. Shower. Major BRAND returned from Course. Att.	M.M.05411 /20000
	24/6/18		Went to visit Coys Behind at PRESSY N, not in afternoon. Att.	
	25/6/18		D Coy moved to HANSON CAMP. Fine. Bat had ABBOTT, MM & Lt. G XVIII Corps went round Camp. Major CRAWFURD returns from temporary command of K.O.S.B. All Coys digging protection for huts. Very good. Att.	
	26/6/18		Day fine. All Coys digging in huts. Major BRAND & O.C. Coys went up to see line held by 7th S.R. who we are to relieve on 29th. Att. Major CRAWFURD left Bat for Senior Officers Course Aldershot Hall.	
	27/6/18		Fine. A.D.T party C tested on gun. Rifle shots at ST. ELOI Bn tgts. w/w Guards, Grenade Throwing, Lewis Guns, Cooking, Football v Cobnon events. Att.	Att. No. 5.
	28/6/18		16 Gunners from U.K leave. C Coy w/b tested on gas where warned for relief of Att.	
	29/6/18		Relieved 7th S.R. in support to left section of Divisional Sector relief complete 1530. Lt. MILNE to Hospital. 30 Men to hospital with Influenza. Capt CURRIE in charge of machine. Major BRAND Commands Both when in support. Lt. Col A. WILSON's Au BOIS. Att.	
VIMY	30/6/18		Major BRAND inspected line held by 4 O/R Coys & advised any dispositions & suggested improvements. Day fine & hot.	
			Killed (accidentally during month) 1 O/R	
			Wounded 6 "	
			" Self inflicted 3 "	

A. Wilson Lt Col

5th BATTALION HIGHLAND LIGHT INFANTRY.

APP. I

Order No. 3.

Reference: MAROEUIL, 1/20000   1st June, 1918.

1. **INFORMATION.** The 157th Infantry Brigade will relieve the 156th Infantry Brigade in the Right WILLERVAL Section of the Divisional Sector on 2nd June.

2. **INTENTION.** The 5th H.L.I. will relieve the 4th Royal Scots, who are holding the Right Sub-section in the Right Sector of the Divisional Sector from TIRED ALLEY inclusive to WESTERN ROAD inclusive;

3. **ORDERS TO TROOPS.**

    (A) The following will be the disposition of Companies:-

    "A" Coy. will relieve "A" Coy. 4th Royal Scots.
    "B" "   "   "   "C" "   do.
    "D" "   "   "   "D" "   do.
    "C" "   "   "   "B" "   do.   in the
    Posts DURHAM, SUBURBS, FOVENT, BARNSLEY.
    One Coy. 7th H.L.I. will relieve "C" Coy. 7th Scottish Rifles:

    The 5 sections of Coy. 7th H.L.I. will take over the Posts in TIRED ALLEY letters "A" to "E" from 5 sections 7th Scottish Rifles.

    One Coy. 7th H.L.I., less 2 platoons, will take over the Post WILLERVAL NORTH; 3 sections 7th H.L.I. will take over VANCOUVER POST.

    (B) Order of March:-

    "D" Coy., "B" Coy., "A" Coy., "C" Coy., Headquarters, 7th H.L.I. Coy.

    The Orders with regard to embussing and debussing will be issued when received from the Brigade.

    (C) Companies will proceed from the debussing point (about 1000 yards West of LE TILLEULS cross-roads) by sections at 150 paces distant via LENS-ARRAS ROAD to TIRED ALLEY Communication Trench.

4. **GUIDES.** The 7th Scottish Rifles will supply a chain of picquets from the debussing point to the junction of TIRED ALLEY and

THELUS RIDGE line.
    One guide per Coy. of the 4th Royal Scots will meet Coys. at the junction of TIRED ALLEY with BROWN LINE.
    The 4th Royal Scots will station Runners at all cross trenches in order to avoid sections going astray.

5. **RELIEF.** Relief will be carried out by daylight. Times will be notified later.
    As the garrisons of WILLERVAL NORTH and VANCOUVER POST cannot take over by daylight, these garrisons will be led on arrival to the Post Line, where they will remain until dark.
    The completion of Relief will be wired to Headquarters by the code word "NEBI".

6. **ADVANCE PARTIES.** The following Advance Parties will be sent to the 4th Royal Scots.

    (a) On 1st June, Signalling Officer, 2 headquarters Signallers, and one Signaller per Coy.; The Officer i/c Regimental Scouts, one N.C.O., and 6 Snipers and Observers; one N.C.O. and 4 Other Ranks per Coy.

    (b) On 2nd June, one Officer per Coy., the R.S.M., L.G.O., and the Battalion Gas N.C.O. This Party will leave LANCASTER CAMP at 8 a.m. Transport Officer will supply horses. This party will take over Area Stores.

7. **BAGGAGE.** No blankets will be taken. Officers will not take valises. Dixes and part of Officers' Mess baggage will be sent to Headquarters 4th Royal Scots on night of 1st June. The Transport Officer will arrange. One batman of Headquarters and one cook will accompany this baggage.
    The remainder of the Regimental baggage will be transferred to the new Regimental Dump at BERTHONVAL FARM. Officers' baggage and men's packs on 1st June; the men's blankets, the Quarter-master's Stores, etc., on morning of 2nd June.

8. **STORES.** The following Regimental Stores will be exchanged with the 4th Royal Scots. "Q" Branch will arrange.

    S.A.A. in boxes.
    Mobile equipment of bombs.
    Establishment of picks and shovels.
    Very Lights.

    The L.G.O. will arrange to exchange all Lewis Gun magazines and tin boxes. Each Lewis Gun Team will carry 8 drums in buckets. Tins for these buckets will be sent, under arrangement to be made by the L.G.O., to BERTHONVAL FARM. Four anti-aircraft Lewis Guns will go with the Battalion nucleus.

9. **TRANSPORT.** The Transport will move to BERTHONVAL FARM under arrangements to be made by the B.T.O.

10. **DRESS.** Fighting Order, with Greatcoat rolled on waist belt.

11. **PARADE.** The hour of Parade will be notified later.

12. **RATIONS.** The rations will be divided to Coys. and sent by Transport Officer on the pack mules to Battalion Headquarters and WILLERVAL. Two Quarter-master Sergeants will accompany the rations each night.
    The rations for Headquarters Coy., and "C" Coy. holding the Post Line, will be drawn from Battalion Headquarters. The rations for the 3 Coys. holding the Front Line will be dumped on the WILLERVAL-ARLEUX ROAD about b.4.c;6.8. One platoon of 7th H.L.I. Coy. holding the BROWN LINE will supply a carrying party to the flank Coys. Each of the flank Coys., "A" and "D", will send 4 men to the Dump to guide and assist the platoon of the 7th H.L.I.. The central Coy., "B", will draw their rations without assistance.

13. **WATER.** Water is conveyed in petrol tins from LONGWOOD by parties supplied by the 7th H.L.I. Coy. in BROWN LINE. Water for the Post Line and "C" and Headquarters Coys. will be brought up by trolley. For the forward Coys. tins are carried by hand. A double supply of petrol tins will be taken over. This will allow the carrying party to always take down at night empty tins. Great care must be taken that no tins are lost or mislaid.

14. **COOKING.** Cooking for the front line Coys. is restricted. The bacon will be cooked at the Quarter-master's Dump and re-heated in the Coy. Cookhouses. Fresh meat will be similarly treated.

15. **TRENCH STANDING ORDERS.** All ranks are referred to Battalion Trench Standing Orders.

16. **Q.M. DUMP.** The personnel of the Quarter-master's Dump will proceed to BERTHONVAL FARM on 2nd June, leaving LANCASTER CAMP at 10 a.m. The Quarter-master will arrange to leave one Coy. Quarter-master Sergeant to hand over the Camp and Regimental Stores to the representative of the 4th Royal Scots. The Quarter-master will send receipts for the Stores handed over to Battalion Headquarters on 3rd June.

17. **BATTALION NUCLEUS.** The Battalion nucleus, under Major Craufurd, will proceed on 2nd June to RISPIN CAMP, VILLERS-au-BOIS. Lieut. Girvan will report at Camp Commandant's Office, VILLERS, at 10 a.m. on 2nd June to take over the Battalion Area. The nucleus will parade at 10 a.m. Transport Officer will supply 2 limbers for baggage.

One Field Kitchen and one Water Cart will accompany this party. Transport Officer will arrange.

18. **FIELD KITCHENS.** Three Field Kitchens and one Water Cart will be taken to BERTHONVAL FARM. All Field Kitchens and Water Carts will be cleaned and ready to draw out at 9.30 a.m.

19. **BAGGAGE.** All baggage will be stacked outside huts or Messes by 9 a.m. Blankets will be rolled in bundles of 10 ready for loading at 7 a.m.
    Regimental Stores which have to proceed to the line will be taken in the first place to BERTHONVAL FARM and sent up to WILLERVAL on the night of the 3/4th June.

1st June, 1918.   Lieut.,
                                       Acting Adjutant 5th H.L.I.

```
Copy No.  1     "A" Coy.
  "   "   2     "B"  "
  "   "   3     "C"  "
  "   "   4     "D"  "
  "   "   5     H.Q. "
  "   "   6     O.i/c Transport.
  "   "   7     Q.M.
  "   "   8     Adjutant.
  "   "   9     7th H.L.I.
  "   "  10     Second in Command.
  "   "  11)
  "   "  12)    Diary.
```

8th Battn. H.L.I.

WARNING ORDER. No 8.

APP III

12th June, 1918.

1. **INFORMATION.** A relief within the Brigade will probably take place on 14th June, 1918.

11. **INTENTION.** The 8th H.L.I. will relieve the 7th H.L.I. in the Right of the Line, WILLERVAL SECTOR Right Sub Sector.

111. **ORDERS TO TROOPS.** Relief, Routes, and Guides as under:—

8th H.L.I.	Relieve 7th H.L.I.	Route.	Time.	Guides.	Guides for 7th H.L.I.
"A"	"A"	TIRED ALLEY.	0800	Junction of Brown L. TIRED ALLEY.	AT SPUR POST 1 for each Post at 2100.
"B"	"B"	" "	1400	ditto.	None.
"C"	"C"	MERSEY.	1900	Junction BROWN LINE MERSEY.	None.
"D"	"D"	2 ptns. TIRED ALLEY. 2 ptns. BEEHIVE.	1800	BROWN LINE, TIRED ALLEY. BROWN LINE & BEEHIVE.	None.
"H.Q."	"H.Q."	MERSEY, Brown Line, TIRED ALLEY & POST LINE. 1800.		BROWN LINE & TIRED ALLEY.	None.

4. **MOVEMENT.** Movement will be by sections at a 100 yards distance. Not more than two platoons of each Battalion will be on the move at the same time.

5. **RELIEF COMPLETE.** Will be wired to NEW Battalion Headquarters by priority wire. Code word "DUD".

6. **ADVANCE PARTIES.** The following advance parties will be supplied by 8th H.L.I. on moving on 14th instant:—

    Per Company. 1 Officer.
                  5 N.C.Os. including Coy. Gas N.C.O.
                  2 Signallers.
                  1 Cook.
                  ~~Batmen~~.

all to leave at 0800 under Company arrangement.

    Headquarters. R.S.M.
                  1 N.C.O.
                  2 Signallers.
                  Runners for Relay Post.
                  Battalion Gas N.C.O.

all to leave at 0800.

Signal Station and Relay Posts to be taken over by 1100 and Orderly Room advised.

SCOUTS. 1 Officer 1 N.C.O., and 6 men.
O.Ps. will be taken over at 0800.

L.G.O. Will leave at 0800 and take over Headquarters Area Stores and L.G. Ammunition.

WATER DUTY MEN. Will take over at LONGWOOD at 0800.

7th H.L.I. PARTIES. One Officer and 5 N.C.Os. per Company will leave their Lines at MERK 0800 on 14th instant.

2. **BAGGAGE. Night 13/14th.** Advance baggage will be ready to

Warning order (continued)

load at 2130. ½ Limber per Company will be supplied.

1 Batman per Company and 3 Regimental Police will accompany this baggage and will see it dumped at 7th H.L.I. Hdqrs., WILLERVAL.

Night 14/15th ½ Limber per Company at 2130 will be supplied. 3 Police will accompany this baggage.

8. **AREA STORES.** All Area Stores will be handed over and receipts obtained.

9. **REGIMENTAL STORES.** The following Regimental Stores will be handed over and receipts obtained:-

    Dixies.
    Periscopes (Box)
    Lewis Gun Drums, except 9 per gun which will be carried by teams and A.A. Drums.
    Lewis Gun Tin Boxes.

10. **"A" Coy., 8th H.L.I.** O.C. "A" Company, 8th H.L.I. will arrange to withdraw from BORDER, FARBUS, and TAPE POSTS before dawn on the 14th instant to SPUR POST.

11. **RATIONS.** Same as before.

Meat for consumption by the 8th H.L.I. on the 14th instant will be sent by Q.M., 7th H.L.I., to new Area.
Meat for consumption by the 7th H.L.I. on the 14th will be sent by Q.M., 8th H.L.I., to present area.

12. **WATER.** Same arrangement as before.

13. **DEPARTURE FROM PRESENT AREA.** Companies will wire their departure to present Battalion Headquarters by the code word "OFF".

14. **TRENCH STANDING ORDERS.** The attention of O.C. Companies is drawn to Battalion Trench Standing Orders and 32nd Division Trench Standing Orders.

    Issued to:-
    No 1   "A" Coy.
       2   "B" "
       3   "C" "
       4   "D" "
       5   Sigs., Scouts, and L.O.O.
       6   7th H.L.I.
       7   R.S.M.
       8   File.
       9   File.

    Lieut.,
    Adjt., 8th H.L.I.

For War Diary

5th Bn. H.L.I.

ORDER No 9.

No 89

APP IV

Reference MAREUIL 1/20000.

I. **INFORMATION.** The 155th Brigade will relieve the 157th Brigade in the WILLERVAL SECTION on the 30/31st June, 1918.

II. **INTENTION.** The Battalion will be relieved in the right Sub Section of the WILLERVAL SECTION by the 5th R.S.F. on the 30/31st June. After relief the Battalion will proceed to HILL'S Camp, NEUVILLE St. VAAST.

III. **ORDERS TO TROOPS.** 1. **RELIEF TO COMPANIES.**
"C" Company, 5th H.L.I., will be relieved by "A" Coy. 5th R.S.F.
"B" Company, 5th H.L.I., will be relieved by "D" Coy. 5th R.S.F.
"A" Company, 5th H.L.I., will be relieved by "C" Coy. 5th R.S.F.
"D" Company, 5th H.L.I., will be relieved by "B" Coy. 5th R.S.F.

2. **GUIDES.** O.C. Companies will detail one guide per platoon and O.i/c Headquarters Company two guides. These guides will be at the point where the RAILWAY crosses TIRED ALLEY at times to be notified later.

3. **ROUTE.** The relieving Companies will be guided by the following routes:-
A " " Coy., 5th R.S.F., TIRED ALLEY and YUKON TRENCH. OTTAWA.
D " " " " " TIRED ALLEY and YUKON TRENCH.
C " " " " " TIRED ALLEY.
B " " " " " TIRED ALLEY, POST LINE.
"HQ" " " " " TIRED ALLEY, POST LINE.

4. **TIMES.** Times of relief will be notified later.

5. **HANDING OVER.** All Trench Stores, etc., will be handed over to relieving unit and receipts obtained
Companies will hand over the following Regimental Stores and obtain receipts.
Lewis Gun Magazines (except 8 per gun and 8 Anti Aircraft drums which will be carried)
Lewis Gun Tin Cases.
Dixies.
Box Periscopes.

All Lewis Gun Drums must be thoroughly clean before the 30th instant.

6. **ADVANCE PARTY.** Advance party from the relieving Battalion will arrive on the 19th June. O.C. Companies will detail one guide to be at Battalion Headquarters at 3 p.m. on 19th instant, to guide Company Advance parties to Company Hdqrs.
O.i/c Regimental Scouts will detail one guide to be at 157th Brigade Headquarters at 3 p.m. on 19th inst. to guide Advance party of relieving Battalion to Battalion Hdqrs.

7. **COMMUNICATIONS.** The N.C.O. i/c Regimental Signals will arrange to hand over Signal Offices and relay Posts by 11 a.m., 30th June. He will report to the Adjutant when this has been done.

8. **OBSERVATION POSTS.** The O.i/c Regimental Scouts will arrange to have the O.Ps. relieved by 6 a.m. on 30th instant. He will report when this has been done.

111. ORDERS TO TROOPS. (contd).

9. **RELIEF COMPLETE.** Relief complete will be wired to Battalion Headquarters by priority wire. Code word "BILLING".

10. **MARCHING OUT.** On relief Companies will proceed independently to HILL'S CAMP, NEUVILLE St. VAAST. The following routes will be used:-

"C" Company, MERSEY ALLEY and tracks to the NEUVILLE St. VAAST LES TILLEULS ROAD.

"B", "A", "D", and H.Q. Companies, By TIRED ALLEY, THEYLUS RIDGE, and thence by tracks to LENS ARRAS ROAD and from there by track to the NEUVILLE St VAAST LES TILLEULS ROAD.

All Companies are warned to avoid the CANADIAN MONUMENT. O.i/c Regimental Scouts will arrange to provide a chain of picquets from Junction THEYLUS RIDGE and TIRED ALLEY to the LENS ARRAS ROAD.

Companies on leaving the communication trench must move in sections at not less than 100 yards interval. This interval will not be closed until Companies arrive at NEUVILLE St. VAAST.

Company Commanders are reminded that the strictest march discipline must be observed and no straggling allowed.

11. **DRESS.** Fighting kit with Greatcoat rolled on waist belt. S.B.R. at the alert.

12. **ARRIVAL AT CAMP.** Each Company and platoon will be met on arrival at Camp by a guide provided from the training Nucleus who will conduct them to their huts. O.C. Companies will report their arrival to the Orderly Room at HILL'S CAMP.

13. **ADVANCE PARTY.** Each Company will send to HILL'S CAMP on the morning of the 20th June at a time to be notified later the following Advance party:-

1 Officer.
4 N.C.Os.
1 Cook.
2 Batmen.
1 Mess Waiter.

Headquarters Company will send

1 Officer.
1 N.C.O.
1 Cook.
Officers' Cook and Mess Waiter.
2 Batmen.
1 Sergeant and 4 rank and file Pioneers.
1 N.C.O. and 2 Signallers.

14. **BAGGAGE.** All baggage not absolutely necessary will be sent down to HILL'S CAMP on the night of 19/20th June.

O.i/c Regimental Transport will arrange to send to WILLERVAL on that night 2½ limbers which will give each Coy. and Headquarters Company ½ Limber.

Front Line Companies will dump their baggage where the WILLERVAL ROAD crosses the YUKON TRENCH. "D" Company and Headquarters will dump their baggage where the WILLERVAL ROAD crosses the POST LINE.

Baggage to be dumped by 10 p.m.

The Assistant Adjutant will arrange to send up with the limbers one man from each Company

On night 20/21st all baggage not sent down on the previous night will be removed by Regimental Transport. Each Coy. and Headquarters will leave one man to look after the baggage and see it loaded.

III. ORDERS TO TROOPS. (contd).

15. **TRANSPORT.** The Regimental Transport will move to its new Lines under arrangements to be made by the B.T.O. Field Kitchens will be taken to HILL'S CAMP but not used.

16. **Q.M. DUMP.** The Quartermaster will arrange to exchange the following regimental stores:-

> S.A.A.
> Grenades.
> Picks.
> Shovels.
> Very Lights.
> Box Periscopes.

All clothing and stores will be transferred under arrangements to be made by the Quartermaster with relieving unit to new Camp. The move to be completed by 12 midday, 20th June.

17. **NUCLEUS.** The O.i/c Nucleus will arrange to march his party to HILL'S CAMP to arrive there by 11 a.m. on 20th June. Separate instructions have been issued to him.

18. **RATIONS.** Rations drawn on the 19th for consumption on the 20th will be sent as usual to WILLERVAL except the meat ration which will be taken under Q.M's arrangement to HILL'S CAMP.

19. **TAKING OVER CAMP.** The Assistant Adjutant will take over from the 5th R.S.F., HILL'S CAMP, and allot quarters. He will arrange to inspect Camp prior to the 20th and send to Battalion Headquarters detail of his allotments of quarters.

20. **REGIMENTAL PRISONERS.** The Regimental prisoners will be sent down on the morning of 20th June. The Corporal in charge of escort will report on arrival to the Assistant Adjutant at HILL'S CAMP

                                                                  Lieut.,
                                                           Adjutant, 5th H.L.I.

18th June, 1918.

Copy No 1. O/C Nucleus Camp.
       2. Q.M. and T.O.
       3. Sig Scout and L.G. Off.
       4. OC A Coy
       5. OC B Coy
       6. OC C Coy
       7. OC D Coy
       8. M/Adj
       9. File
      10. File
      11. 5 R.S.F.

5th H. L. I.

ORDER No 10.

Copy No 12.
APP V

Reference BAROEUIL 1/20000.

I. INFORMATION. The 157th Infantry Brigade will relieve the 156th Infantry Brigade in the ~~reserve area near VIMY~~ left CHAUDIERE section on ~~29th~~ 30th June.

II. INTENTION. The 5th H. L. I. will relieve the 7th Scottish Rifles.

III. ORDERS TO TROOPS. The following will be the disposition of the Companies:-

"D" Company will relieve "A" Company, 7th Scottish Rifles.
"C"   "   "   "D"   "   "   "
"A"   "   "   "B"   "   "   "
"B"   "   "   "C"   "   "   "

(b) ROUTE. "H.Q.", "D" and "C" Companies will march from HILLS Camp to the barrier on the LaFOLIE FARM Road, the leading platoon arriving there at 12.15 p.m.
Order of March: "D", "C", "H.Q."
The leading platoon will leave HILLS Camp at 11.45 a.m.

(c) "A" and "B" Companies will march via the ARRAS-SOUCHEZ Road, and CAMPBELL Road to S.28.a.3.6., the leading platoon arriving there at 12.15 p.m.
Order of March: "A" Company, "B" Company.
The leading platoon will leave HILLS Camp at 11.45 a.m.

(d) GUIDES. One Officer and one other rank per Battalion Headquarters, one Officer per Company and one other rank per platoon will meet Headquarters, "D" and "C" Companies at the barrier S.28.d.6.6. at 12.15 p.m., and "A" and "B" Companies on CAMPBELL Road S.28.a.3.6. at 12.15 p.m.

(e) "H.Q.", "D" and "C" Companies will move by HUMBER Trench, and "A" and "B" Companies by BLIGHTY Trench.
Up to the VIMY RIDGE, movement will be by platoons at 200 yards distance; after that it will be by groups of two sections at 100 yards distance.

(f) ∧advance party One Signaller per Company and two from Battalion Headquarters will be at the barrier at S.28.d.6.6. at 3 p.m. to-day to meet guides from the 7th Scottish Rifles.

(g) ADVANCE PARTY. Advance party consisting of Battalion Intelligence Officer, one Officer per Company, one N.C.O. per platoon and Company Gas N.C.Os. will move in advance of the battalion on the 29th, leaving HILLS camp at 9 a.m.

11. ORDERS TO TROOPS. (contd)

(g) ADVANCE PARTY. The Officer per Company will take over trench stores, carefully inspecting them before taking over.

(h) DRESS. Fighting Order with greatcoat rolled on belt.

(i) RATIONS. Rations will be divided to Companies and sent direct by the Quartermaster to Companies.
Rations for "A" and "B" Companies will be sent by Light Railway to CAYUGA dump (S.24.c.6.2.)
"C" Company to BORDON dump (T.25.a.4.6.)
"D"   "   to NEW BRUNSWICK (T.19.d.8.2.)
"H.Q." by Limber.

(j) Rations for consumption to-morrow. The bread ration will be issued to-morrow, and tea at 11 a.m. Meat for consumption to-morrow will be sent to the new area to-night by 2½ Limbers; also Officers' packs, one batman and one cook per Company to accompany the limbers.

(k) WATER PICQUETS. "D" Company will supply a picquet of 1 N.C.O. and 4 Men to GOODMAN MAIN and VIMY. (T.20.c.3.1.)
"C" Company will supply a Water Picquet of 1 N.C.O. and 3 Men to GIVENCHY (S.12.b.9.6.), (S.12.b.6.5.), and VIMY (S.18.c.9.3.) (S.24.b.2.9.)

(L) RESERVE RATIONS. The following reserve rations will be taken over:-

		S.24.d.1.2.	Biscuits.	750.	Meat	756.
"D" Company,		T.7.d.9.5.	"	1350.	"	1338.
-do-		T.21.a.3.3.	"	600.	"	576.

(m) SALVAGE. The sections of "C" Company will parade at 10 a.m. on 30th instant for Salvage duty at VICTORIA dump.
Salvage dumps are at VICTORIA, CAYUGA and PEGGY.

(n) TRENCH STANDING ORDERS. All ranks are referred to battalion and divisional Trench Standing Orders.

(o) REGIMENTAL AID POST. The Aid Post will be near Battalion Headquarters on the EAST of the LENS-ARRAS Road.

(p) LEWIS GUN ANTI-AIRCRAFT POSTS. The L.G.O. will detail 1 N.C.O. and 6 Men from Headquarters Company to provide an anti-aircraft gun post near Battalion Headquarters and a post with "D" Company. Three of these will be attached to "D" Company for rations.

(q) COMMUNICATIONS. 1.

over/

111. ORDERS TO TROOPS. (contd)

(q) COMMUNICATIONS. (1) The Signalling Officer will take over from the 7th Scottish Rifles:-

    2 Fuller phones.
    1 Buzzer unit.
    1 Power buzzer and Amplifier.

He will hand over to the 7th Scottish Rifles:-

    1 Fuller phone.
    1 Magneto telephone.

(2) The Signalling Officer will arrange to man the power buzzer and amplifier station at Headquarters with trained personnel presently attached.

(3) Transport telephone will be manned by three signallers to be detailed by the Signalling Officer. The Assistant Adjutant will arrange for one Orderly to be stationed at the Signal Office for duty.

(4) The Signalling Officer will detail one visual signaller and three runners to report to Brigade Headquarters at 10 a.m. on 30th inst.

(5) RELAY POSTS. The Signalling Officer will arrange for relay post No.1 to be taken over at old Brigade Headquarters in La FOLIE COPS (S.03.0.3.0.) with six men, and to provide two men for post No.2 at Battalion Headquarters in Sunken Road.

(6) Signalling Officer will detail pigeoneer to report at Brigade Headquarters at 10 a.m. daily to take pigeons to No.2 Post.

(7) Any existing rocket station and supply of rockets will be taken over by units in whose area they are.

    Copy No. 1   O.C. "A" Coy.
              2   " "B" "
              3   " "C" "
              4   " "D" "
              5   O1/C L.G.O., Sigs., Scouts.
              6   O.C. 7th Scottish Rifles.
              7   Transport Officer.
              8   Quartermaster.
              9   Second in Command.
            10   Adjutant.
           11)
           12) File.

David E. Brand Lyon
Lieut.,

5th H. L. I.

ADMINISTRATIVE INSTRUCTIONS FOR ORDER No 10.

1. **REGIMENTAL STORES.** The following regimental stores will be handed over to a representative of the 7th Scottish Rifles and a receipt obtained.

   - 76 boxes S.A.A.
   - 36 " Grenades.
   - 110 Shovels.
   - 76 Picks.

   The Quartermaster will arrange to hand over and will draw the same stores from the 7th Scottish Rifles at DALY Camp. The Quartermaster will hand over 33 Camp kettles.

2. **DUMP.** The Quartermaster's dump will be situated at DALY Camp as from 29th June inclusive.

3. The following personnel will form the Quartermaster's dump:-

	Officers.	N.C.Os.	Rank & File.
Stores.	2	2	1
Cobblers.	-	-	3
Butchers.	-	-	2
Tailors.	-	-	4
Officers Mess	-	-	1
C.Q.M.S.	-	4	-
Barber.	-	-	1
Sergeant Drummer	-	1	-
Runners	-	-	2
Pioneers.	-	-	2
Canteen	-	1	1
Orderly Room.	1	1	1
Armourer.	-	-	1
Postman	-	-	1
Batmen	-	-	3
Cooks	-	2	7
Working Party.	-	1	4
Water-duty men.	-	-	2
	3	12	36

The Quartermaster will hand to Orderly Room by 5 p.m. on 28th June duplicate nominal roll of the above party.

The above party will parade on 29th instant at 10 a.m. in Marching Order, and will be marched to the dump by the Assistant Adjutant.

4. **BAGGAGE.** The Quartermaster will arrange to transfer to his dump as much baggage as possible on the 28th June. The balance of baggage will be taken on the morning of 29th June; the battalion dump to be cleared by 10 a.m.

5. **WORKSHOPS.** The battalion workshops will close at 12 noon on 28th June, and will re-open at Quartermaster's dump at 12 noon on 29th June.

6. CANTEEN/

ADMINISTRATIVE INSTRUCTIONS FOR ORDER No 10 (contd).

6. **CANTEEN.** The battalion canteen will close at 6 p.m. on 28th.

7. **PACKS.** Packs will be stacked by Companies on battalion parade ground under arrangements to be made by the Quartermaster with Company Quartermaster Sergeants before 4 p.m. 28th June.

8. **OFFICERS' BAGGAGE.** Officers' baggage not required for the line will be stacked on battalion parade ground by Officers' servants before 4 p.m. on 28th June.

9. **KITCHENS.** The Quartermaster will arrange that field kitchens are ready to pull out at 9 a.m., 28th June.

10. **WATER CARTS.** The Quartermaster will arrange that Water Carts are ready to pull out at 9 a.m. 28th June.

11. **TECHNICAL STORES.** The Regimental Sergeant Major will issue the following stores to Companies before 4 p.m. on 28th June, obtaining receipts for issues:-
    For each Company. 12 Wire Cutters.
    -                  12 pairs Hedging Gloves.
    -                  12 Small Periscopes.
    -                  5 Very Pistols.
    -                  6 Gratade Guns.
    -                  12 Haversack Grenade Carriers.
    -                  6 Belt Grenade Carriers.
    The following stores will be taken up to line by R.S.M.
    -                  9 Range Finders.
    -                  Figure Targets.
    -                  Patrol Hats.
    -                  Wire Cutters, Rifle.
    -                  Hand barrows.

    The balance of R.S.M's dump will be handed to Quartermaster on 28th June and receipts obtained.

12. **BADGES.** The Quartermaster will arrange to issue to Companies before 4 p.m. on 28th June eight runners badges per Company and 12 to Headquarters.

13. **TRANSPORT.** The Transport Officer will arrange direct with the Quartermaster for transport necessary to move stores to the new dump at DALE CAMP. The move of the transport will be carried out under orders of the B.T.O.

14. **NUCLEUS.** Captain A.S.Currie will be in command of the battalion nucleus. He will be handed by the Orderly Room by 12 noon on 28th instant nominal roll of all ranks forming the nucleus.
    The following is the staff which he will have under his command:-   1 C.S.M.
                         4 Cooks.
                         2 Lewis Gun Instructors.
                         1 Grenade Instructor.
                         1 Musketry Instructor.

ADMINISTRATIVE INSTRUCTIONS FOR ORDER No 10 (contd).

Nucleus will parade on 29th June at 9 a.m. in Marching Order, and will proceed to the Nucleus Camp, VILLERS AU BOIS reporting their arrival to the Commandant, Divisional Reception Camp.

The Orderly Room will arrange to give the ration strength to the Quartermaster.

O.C. Nucleus is responsible that any change in the personnel is notified to the Assistant Adjutant immediately at the dump. This change should be notified in duplicate.

The Assistant Adjutant will, when sending any ranks to the nucleus, notify O.C. Nucleus in order that this Officer may keep his rolls correct.

15. COMMUNICATIONS. The N.C.O. in charge of signals will arrange that the nucleus take with them two bicycles; that five bicycles are left at the dump; and that two bicycles will proceed with the battalion to the line.

16. HANDING OVER CAMP. The Assistant Adjutant will arrange to hand over EILEN AND NEWTON CAMPS with Defence Schemes, Plan of Camps and other papers to representative 7th Scottish Rifles. The Fire Orders hung up in each hut will be handed to Orderly Room by 8 a.m 29th June, and handed by Assistant Adjutant to 7th Scottish Rifles

                                                           Lieut.,

27th June, 1918.   A/Adjutant, 5th K.L.I.

File.

5th Bn H.L.I.

War Diary

No 38

Volume I

July, 1918.

Army Form C. 2118.

WAR DIARY
or
INTELLIGENCE SUMMARY.

38/1

3rd H.L.I.

(Erase heading not required.)

Place	Date	Hour	Summary of Events and Information	Remarks and references to Appendices
VIMY	1/7/18		Went round wire of Battn sector in BROWN LINE from LENS-ARRAS ROAD to right of sector with R.E. and M.G. Officers. Arranged what wiring had to be done. Inspected B. Coys. Hqrs. and position of aforesaid Platoon in CYMBAL TRENCH. Capt. PARR reported that he had only two Platoons in LA CHAUDIERE instead of three as he had previous that he had occupied the day as his third Platoon were to have used & infested with influenza. Sent orders to M.O. to inspect and report.	MORBOURG 1/2/0000
	2/7/18		That O.C. 6th H.L.I. and made provisional arrangements regarding relief. O.C. Coys visited areas they will be taking over. Transferred 10 boxes S.A.A. from S. Lilet S.A.A. in C. Coys area to trench Reserve of B. Coy. R.W.	
	3/7/18		Received Brigade Orders that we would relieve 6th H.L.I. on 5th inst. Accompanied by 6 H.L.I. Hqrs. and completed arrangements for relief. Platoon commanders visited areas they are to take over. MS	
	4/7/18		Conference of Coy. Commanders in forenoon, explained definitions of Coys. in BETTY AREA & the arrangements to take over and the best to for reconnoitering positions for our Platoon Hqrs. in near of BLACK LINE and for having accommodation for one third Platoon in the BLACK LINE. Orders for 4 o. Bear Attack on 5/7/18. Most suitable light guns over. To B.G. R.E. VIII Corps recommended ground behind BROWN LINE and explained that this area, on the forward of present trench held by eastern Platoon in "BM" trs. appeared that the airplane to one at a two Craned worked on these by day. MS	

Army Form C. 2118.

WAR DIARY
or
INTELLIGENCE SUMMARY.
(Erase heading not required.)

38/2

5th H.L.I.

Instructions regarding War Diaries and Intelligence Summaries are contained in F. S. Regs., Part II. and the Staff Manual respectively. Title pages will be prepared in manuscript.

Place	Date	Hour	Summary of Events and Information	Remarks and references to Appendices
VIMY	5.7.18		Relieved 6th H.L.I. in left subsection of left sector (BETTY subsection). Relief complete 1110. Orders for two coys issued. Bn. HQ formed. All quiet. Went round line. Patrol under Lt TURNBULL found no trace of enemy patrol.	Manoeuvre 12000 Appendix No 1. "2
	6/7/18		Front line still quiet. Went round line. 2nd Lieut. Capt HORNE for A/C Coy. Patrols under Lt SWEET (B Coy) & 2/Lt SPEIR DCASON (C Coy), nothing to report. Night quiet.	
	7/7/18		2nd Day quiet. Enemy aeroplane brought down in morning at LA CHAUDIERE. Patrol Lt POAK nothing to report. Jopling reported in HQ Coy Hone when on on a slight alignment Canadian tunnelling Coy Coal shield Sapper to listen. Capt CURRIE went on home leave pm Patrol B Coy. nothing to report. Night quiet.	
	8/7/18		First Act. Day quiet. R.E.'s & new Adj Major around line. Chos new Capt Horne for D Coy. Patrol B Coy nothing to report night quiet.	
	9/7/18		First in morning - Small Shoony in afternoon. Enemy aeroplane brought down about FOR B.W.S. Enemy shelled vicinity of Both Hymn at 0830 4 guns at 2100 - 1 o/r. Wounded. About 2300 R.H.A line shelled. Casualties S o/r 20.	

A 5834 Wt. W 4973/M687 750,000 8/16 D. D. & L. Ltd. Forms/C. 2118/13.

Army Form C. 2118.

WAR DIARY
or
INTELLIGENCE SUMMARY.
(Erase heading not required.)

5th A.2.1.

30/2.

Place	Date	Hour	Summary of Events and Information	Remarks and references to Appendices
VIMY.	10.7.16		Lt. Col. NEILSON left Batt. Hdqrs. & proceeded on special leave. Have Major BRAND assumed command. Very dull and showery. Men went round BLACK LINE and BLUE LINE. Capt. WATSON took over command of "B" Coy. from Capt. MORRISON who had to proceed to details. 2. Lt. HARPE left to attend a 53 Gen. Course in G.S.R. and 2 Lt. WILLIAMSON Capt. MILLER returned from attack. 2nd Lt. McKIE from Hospital. Casual Shelling. Casualties 1 wounded. BVB been evacuated to Hospital.	
	9.7.16		Very showery. Report received from O.C. "A" Company. Trenches bag. Not at to day but Lt. TEDDIE GERARD nor KEENE who taking up returned have been in listeners were posted for these nights and that his further counts on 6.7.16. could be withstood an enemy counter was heard. Not content to return to reinforce Brigade remonstrated with O.C. "B" Coy. (Lt. CARMICHAEL) in turn to order to PICTON TRENCH and that further his RED TRENCH from PICTOV TRENCH to be on Watson ARRAS ROAD to move into after receipt of RED TRENCH to "Watson" on "B" Coy. to order "Pature" for attack. Informed by D Coy. in VESTA TILLEY and TOLEDO TRENCHES and expected S.O.S. Passed by D. Coy. between the heavy showers. B.M. O.P. in VESTA TILLEY. Observation only good from BLUE Orders received from Brigade stopping to move night Patrons "B" Coy. to enter to night and LINE to RED TRENCH, left platoon "B" Coy. the two platoons B (S) coy. in the BLUE Orderly sector formerly held by two platoons B (S) coy. tomorrow. LINE. Move the complete by 0900 tomorrow. Was received that info forwards (Lt. Gen. HUNTER WESTON) will visit Batt of line tomorrow. BVB	

A 5834 Wt. W4973/M687 750,000 8/16 D. D. & L. Ltd. Forms/C.2118/13.

WAR DIARY
INTELLIGENCE SUMMARY

Army Form C. 2118.

5th H.L.I.

38/4.

Place	Date	Hour	Summary of Events and Information	Remarks and references to Appendices
VIMY	12/7/16		Any stationary. Lad. with Lt. CARMICHAEL D.S.O., went out on patrol to reconnoitre the wire in front of enemy trenches S.W. of MERICOURT at T.N.C.O.P. Strength of patrol 1 officer, 2 B.M. Scouts, 2 rifle bombers and 1 Lewis Gun team. On reaching a suitable place the main body was left as a covering party, whilst Lt. CARMICHAEL and the 2 B.M. Scouts crawled forward to examine the wire. When they were near the reconnoitring party began to withdraw to the covering party, and at once was attacked by the enemy, estimated strength 10-15. Lt. CARMICHAEL met the numbers and cock of the events, three 3 bombers in the middle of the enemy who were seen by the light from enemy flares the about 20 yards away, at the moment one of the enemy (L" 20024 Pt. D PIRIE) was seized by the throat by a German, but he managed to stab his opponent in the throat by with his bayonet; the German fell dying down dead as the others closed came up to assist. The enemy patrol was now disorganised and the awate patrol withdrew without further interference to the covering party, which then came back through our wire enemy shortly after daybreak. The army were evidently carried by scouts detached from covering patrols as bayonet and hills wounds only, the rifle being too bulky, should withstand patrol. But enemy Attempted counts hunted at FORT GEORGE. The Corps Commander inspected the BLACK LINE held by the Batt., Capt. PARR in command for the day.	

A 5834 Wt. W 4973/M687. 750,000 8/16 D.D. & L. Ltd. Forms/C.2118/13.

Army Form C. 2118.

WAR DIARY
or
INTELLIGENCE SUMMARY.

5th H.L.I.

Place	Date	Hour	Summary of Events and Information	Remarks and references to Appendices
VIMY.	12.7.16 (cont.)		CAPT MILLER took over temporary command by C. Coy. Capt STRACHAN left bn marketing course — Casualties 1 wounded. 343.	
	12.7.16		A gas alarm attack was delivered this morning at 0220. The Brickeys Point being from our S.O.S. line at TOLEDO TRENCH. A similar attack was launched from a Brickeys Point to the crew by the 6th H.L.I. on our right. The Infantry 1050 to wounded were brought up on imaginary drawn to a Ridhland to front by the BLUE LINE from then 10 parties & 20 each, provided by the Batt. in reserve finished them (5 trucks for party) to the Brickeys Point. & knives here were supplied by no tram. The house of the discharge and of the trades. We go was discharged without incident. After the gas attack on your attack heavily. And the enemy retaliated on our line. Casualties killed 4, wounded 1. N° 201732 Cpl. H. FRICKER and 7333 4/c M. MACPHERSON both b B. Coy. were Killed in the RUE LINE. N° 200270 Pt. DONALD PIRIE in military held to his work on patrol but over left part of BLACK LINE and RED TRENCH Recommended on wight of 11/12th July. The Adjutant Lt. CLARKE exchanged duties for a few days with W. LEGATE Asst Adjutant at Transport lines. DM5	

WAR DIARY or INTELLIGENCE SUMMARY

Army Form C. 2118.

5th H.L.I.   38/6.

Place	Date	Hour	Summary of Events and Information	Remarks and references to Appendices
VIMY	14.7.16		Reference patrol (D Coy) a Cpl & 4 men. Stopped "C" enemy patrol (about 8) but moved out & line at Stand to. Checking position & right Platoon of 20th Bn. In afternoon approached GERTIE from our right in LINE to ACTRESS and ADEPT. On enemy reinforced two trenches we may be taken BLACK LINE to PEGGIE as evening set in day. Received 157 Brigade over this post. Scheme of Defence for Brigade area. Recommend Lt. I. CARMICHAEL D.S.O. for Military Cross for work done on patrol on night 11/12 July. BM.	Appendix No.3 No.4
	15.7.16		Warte & manual duties. Relief on 17th July, but 2 i/c command & returning went. 5.R.S.F. Trench harrassing by Germans for period in Reserve at PARK undertake. Right Coy of 20 Bn in RED TRENCH west of LENS ARRAS ROAD night rest. BM	
	16.7.16		Thunderstorm in night and in early morning very heavy rain after stood to. Troops & Travel system on not drained in that it a depth of 1 foot. Patrol of T.4.18.4.00 to first shells buried in water at distance of 750 yds. did not find the Johan cushion but lay of or rafts on in enemy had O.C. "B" Battalion on night -4. Royal Scots determined. Survey in current disposition. BM	
FRASER CAMP ST. ELOI/1.	17.7.16		Relieved by 5th R.S.F. Billy collected at 1600. Battalion marched from enlisting hunts by berries. Half Battalion in FRASER CAMP and half in LANCASTER CAMP. BM	

Army Form C. 2118.

WAR DIARY
or
INTELLIGENCE SUMMARY.

(Erase heading not required.)

5th H.L.I.

38/7.

Place	Date	Hour	Summary of Events and Information	Remarks and references to Appendices
FRASER CAMP ST. ERY.	18.7.16		Day spent cleaning hut outfitting camp etc. Lt. W.B. MILNE and 2/Lt. FRASER reporting for duty. Training infantry by Coy. Commanders. Syllabus.	
	19/7/16		Training to programme.	
	20.7.16		Moved to LOZINGHAM by troop train transport by road, orders were to entrain at 13.15. Train 5 hour late, arrived CALONNE RICOUART at 02.45, marched to hut camp in Chateau grounds at LOZINGHAM 4am. I.W.S.	
LOZINGHAM	21/7/16		Lt Col NEILSON returned from Special leave to U.K. a.m.	Fraser Sketch 1 militia
	22/7/16		Inspected huts & arranged for improvements. Coys training. Weather fine raining day between y6ll during night. Lt COTTERELL left to join Air Force field	
	23/7/16		Very wet all day. Received warning that Bde in another Area to be ready tomorrow am to move within y26h. aff	
	24/7/16		All Surplus baggage sent to Bde dump at AUCHEL. Blankets sent to rightening finish. Received Sketches orders for move. OC 4/4/0 Coys reconnoitred LILLERS Area. Say Son's Coys Training. Reinforcing draft of 67 O.R.s of which 46 never-moisey on NB that I approved. at G.S. BASE reported for duty. R.l.l.	Lt Letheton W.5.
	25/7/16		Showery. Projected drafts. Coys training. O.C.s Coys reconnoitred LILLERS Area.	
	26/7/16		Showery MAJOR NEILSON proceeded to 1st Army School commanding Officers Course. Chiefs hand acquired Commandant Rendezvous. C.HQC 01/2S LINE. for programme. Scout 9mies on Range. B/4S.	

WAR DIARY / INTELLIGENCE SUMMARY

Army Form C. 2118

38/5 5th H.T.I.

Place	Date	Hour	Summary of Events and Information	Remarks and references to Appendices
LOZINGHEM	27/7/17		Very heavy rain. Training entailed musketry practice completed by B. Coy. Yks. Capt. V. Chalmers CLARK reported from Egypt. Divine Service.	Appendix No. 6
	28/7/17		Preparing Kit.	
	29/7/17		Training in programme. Warning orders received that XIII Corps will relieve Canadian Corps in ARKAS SECTOR & line the Brown Line taking over the left half Sector, the Bn. to move to BARLIN. Band playing for men. Bns.	
BOIS d'OLHAIN BARLIN	30/7/17		Bn. marched to vicinity of BARLIN, camping for the night in the Bois d'OLHAIN. Went in advance by motor to MAROEUIL, there informed by B.G.C. of area to be taken over by Bgde. and that "Bdr" would hold the BROWN LINE in Bgde. area. Reconnoitred BROWN LINE opposing Bttn. Dvs. Lt. R. L. SWEET M.C. proceeded to England on 12.H.F. 12 miles	
ECURIE WOOD CAMP Nr ROCLINCOURT	31/7/17		Bn. marched from Bois d'OLHAIN to ECURIE WOOD CAMP nr ROCLINCOURT passing starting point at 1230. One hour halt at 1530 for tea, arrived in camp at 1930. Coy. Commanders rode on advance to reconnoitre line. Reported by Bgde. that there was room for only 3 Coys. in an action. An armoured at camp informed by Bgde. that transport lories moved to at ECOIVRE, transport and mobile reserve of S.A.A. to sent there. Dvs.	

WAR DIARY or INTELLIGENCE SUMMARY

Army Form C. 2118.

3819

5 & 172.1

Place	Date	Hour	Summary of Events and Information	Remarks and references to Appendices
ECURIE WOOD CAMP, nr ROCLINCOURT	31/7/18		Increase and Decrease July 1918.	

Increase.
O. ORK
Arrivals (Lt. BARR) 1 73
Rejoined from Hospital. Sick 5 101
" " " Wounded 1
——
6 175

Decrease
O. ORK
To Hospital Sick 2 51
" " Wounded 14
" " Killed 4
To R.A.F. 2
To M.G. Corps. 2
" Communication
" Not increase 104
——
6 175
A.V.S.

5th H. L. I.

Appendix No. 1.

Copy No. 12.

ORDER No 11.

Reference MAROEUIL 1/20000.

1. INFORMATION. The Front Line Left Sub-section of the Left CHAUDIERE Section is held by the 6th H. L. I.

11. INTENTION. The 5th H.L.I. will relieve the 6th H.L.I. on 5th July, 1918, in the Front Line Left Sub-section.

111. ORDERS TO TROOPS. 1. Relief.
"D" Company will relieve "A" Coy. 6th H.L.I. Right Company.
"C" Company, 5th H.L.I. will relieve "B" Coy. 6th H.L.I. Right Centre.
"A" Coy. 5th H.L.I. will relieve "C" Coy. 6th H.L.I. Left Centre.
"B" Coy. 5th H.L.I. will relieve "D" Coy. 6th H.L.I. Left Company.

2. Order of relief. "D" and "C" Companies and "A", "B" and Headquarters Companies will carry out the relief concurrently, commencing with "D" and "A" Companies.

3. Time. The leading Companies, "D" and "A" will move at 0730 on 5th July.

4. Formation. Companies will move in parties of two sections within 100 yards distance.

5. Routes. "D" Company, 2 Platoons by PEGGY-GERTIE- to JAMES trenches, and 2 Platoons by PEGGY to TEDDY trench.
"C" Coy. 2 Platoons by Buster and PEGGY, 2 Platoons by PEGGY-GERTIE- JAMES- HAYTER.
"A" Coy. by GLACE-CENTRE-HALIFAX-BOIS CHAUDIERE- along EMBANKMENT -JULIA -HAYTER.
"B" Coy. by BLIGHTY-GLACE-CENTRE-PICTOU-DARTMOUTH-BETTY- ACTRESS-KEENE.
H.Q. by LENS-ARRAS Road-GLACE-SCOTIA.

6. GUIDES. One Officer per Company and one other rank per platoon will meet Companies as follows:-
"D" and "C" Companies at junction of GERTIE and PEGGY trenches.
"A" "B" and H.Q. Coys. at the crossing of GLACE trench and NANAIMO road.

7. Duties to be taken over from 6th H.L.I.
(a) LAISON posts with 20th Division.
3 LIASON posts will be taken over by "B" Coy. All of these posts will be found by one rifle section for each.
The third on the LENS-ARRAS Road will consist of ½ Lewis Gun section. (1 gun).
(b) Water Picquets. The following picquets will be taken over

(2)

Water Picquets. (contd)

by the water-duty Corporal and water-duty men:-
　　1 N.C.O. and 2 Other ranks over 1-400gln tank at T.8.a.0.0.
　　　　　　　　　　　　　　　　　　4-400gln tank " T.8.a.5.6.
　　　　　　　　　　　　　　　　　　4-400 "   " " T.8.d.5.6.

(c) Observation Post. 4 Battalion Scouts will take over the 2 Observation Posts at dawn on the 5th inst.

(d) Reserve Ration Dump. "C" Coy. will take over and provide a a guard for dump in their area at T.7.d.9.5.

(e) Relay Post at Battalion Hqrs. The Signalling will arrange to relieve the four runners at this post at 12 noon.

8. Duties to be taken over by 6th H.L.I.
(a) The relay post at LA FOLIE COPSE of 1 N.C.O. and 3 men and the relay post of two other ranks at present Batt. Hqrs. will be relieved by the 6th H.L.I. by 0800 on 5th July.
　　The N.C.O. taking over the relay post at LA FOLIE COPSE will also take over the dump there.

(b) Reserve Ration guard at VIMY. (S.24.d.1.2.) This guard will be relieved by the Company taking over from "C" Coy.

(c) Water Picquets. The picquets (of 1 N.C.O. and 4 at GOODMAN MAIN) (T.20.c.3.1.) and VIMY and) of 1 N.C.O. and 3 at GIVENCHY (S.12.b.9.6.) (S.12.b.8.5.) and VIMY (S.18.c.9.3.)(S.24.b.2.9.) will be relieved by the 6th H.L.I. on the morning of 5th July. The relief will report at Batt. Hqrs. at 0630 on 5th July. The scout Officer will detail 2 scouts to guide the relief to their posts.

(d) The Brigade Observation Post will be relieved on the night of 4/5th July.

9. Advance Parties. One Officer per Company, 1 N.C.O. and 1 Lewis Gunner per platoon, 1 other rank per Company, and the Intelligence Officer and 4 scouts from Hqrs. Company will proceed to the respective Companies they are taking over from on the night of 4/5th July after their evening meal.

(b) The Signalling Officer, 3 Hqrs. Signallers and 2 signallers per Company will, on the morning of 5th July, take over Signal Offices. These offices will be taken over at 12.
　　The Signallers will report to the Signalling Officer at the junction of the BROWN LINE and ANGERS Road.
　　The 3 "D" Mark 111 phones at present in the line ("A","B" and "C" Companies) will be taken. Instructions as to the redistribution of phones will be given on arrival of signallers at 6th H.L.I. Hqrs.
　　6 Hqrs runners, as detailed by the Signalling Officer, will proceed with this party to reconnoitre various roads.

10. RATIONS. Rations for consumption on the 5th/6th July will be sent on the night of 4/5th to the present 6th H.L.I. Hqrs. These will be

RATIONS.(contd)

unloaded and carried to Company dumps by parties supplied by 6th H.L.I. and ahnded over to representative from each Coy.

(b) Rations for the 6th H.L.I. for consumption on the 5th of July will be delivered to the companies of the 5th H.L.I. Coys. will provide parties to unload and convey these to their respective Company dumps where they will be handed to a representative of the 6th H.L.I.

(c) From and after the night 5/6th July rations for the whole Battalion will be delivered by rail to VICTORIA Dump near Bn. Hqrs. Each Company will send a carrying party of 1 N.C.O and 12 men nightly at 2130 to unload and carry the rations to their Company Dump. Equipment for this carrying party will be rifle bandolier and S.B.R.

11. WATER. Companies will draw water as follows:
H.Q. Company from tank in T.8.a.00.
"D" and "C" Companies from 4 tanks in T.8.d.5.6.
"A" , "B"   "   "   "   " in T.8.a.7.8.

12. EXCHANGE. 240 Loaded Lewis Gun Magazines per Company and 60 from Hqrs Company will be exchanged (exclusive of the 8 drums per gun to be carried). Tin cases will not be exchanged. Coys will arrange for their empty tin cases being man handled to the new area.

(b) Cooking Utensils. Detchies will be carried by hand. Companies should have 7 each and Hqrs 5.

13. DRESS AND EQUIPMENT. Fighting order with greatcoat rolled on belt.

14. Lewis Gunners will carry 8 drums per gun.

15. Salved Material. The Battalion Salvage Dump will be at VICTORIA Dump near Battalion Hqrs.

16. Battalion Hqrs. will be at T.13.b.5.4.

17. The Regimental Aid Post will be at HAYTER TUNNEL under embankment at T.13.b.6.7.

18. Completion of Relief. Completion of relief will be wired immediately to Headquarters. Code word "KANTARA".

19. Advance Party from 6th H.L.I. One Officer per Company and one from Hqrs Coy. 6th H.L.I. will report to their respective Coys from which they are taking over on the morning of 5th. These Officers will take over Trench and Area Stores. 1 N.C.O. per Coy. will be detailed to hand over these stores and take receipts.

(Sgd) T.B. Clarke. Lieut.,
Adjutant, 5th H. L. I.

3rd July, 1918.

(4)

Copy No 1	O.C. "A" Coy.
2	" "B" "
3	" "C" "
4	" "D" "
5	Oi/c Sigs, Scouts, L.Gs.
6	O.C. 5th H.L.I.
7	Second in Command.
8	Adjutant.
9	T. O.
10	Q.M.
11) 12)	File.

5 H.L.I.

Appendix to War Diary for
July 1915.

6th H. L. I.

Appendix N°2

ORDER No 11.

Copy No 10.

Reference Map 1/20000 MAROEUIL.

1. A Gas Beam Attack will be carried out on the 157th Infantry Brigade Front on the night 5/6th July, 1916, or on first ~~the~~ night after upon which the wind is favourable. The Attack will be in charge of "O" Special Company R.E.

 The Cylinders are to be discharged in any wind between west, nor'west and southwest of a velocity of not less than 6 m.p.h.

2. On the Brigade Front Gas will be discharged from Nos 5 and 6 Railheads.

Line.	Base.	Power Heads.	Discharge Point.	Trucks.	Cylinders
5	Territorial N.of BOURIE.	T.21.c.3.5.	T.16.5.	50	1050.
6	Territorial.	T.14.b.1.0.	T.9.b.	50	1050.

3. The Infantry pushing parties, etc., will be furnished by the 6th H.L.I.

4. O.C. "B" Company will detail one Lewis Gun Section under an Officer to be at the Discharge Point in T.9.B. to cover the noise of the discharge. One gun only will fire; the other being held as a stand by in case of the stoppage of the first gun. The section will be in position at 11 p.m. and fire occasional short bursts. The section will be withdrawn one hour after the trucks have left the discharge Point. Battalion Headquarters will be informed by O.C. "B" Company when the section is in position and when it has been withdrawn.

 If the Officer in charge of the Section hears any noise being made by the trucks moving, he will order short bursts of fire to cover the noise. Care must be taken not to draw the enemy's attention to the fact that ~~nothing~~ anything unusual is going on.

 O.C. "B" Company will arrange that sufficient magazines are taken up with the section to ensure the carrying out of the above orders.

 Box Respirators will be worn by the section from Zero minus two minutes until the area is reported clear by the Battalion Gas N.C.O.

 The Lewis Gun when firing will have only numbers one and two of the team; the remainder of the section will be in touch but under cover.

ORDERS No 11 (contd).

5. O.C. "B" and "D" Companies will arrange to withdraw their Observation sections from TOLEDO trench before Zero hour into BETTY Trench and VESTA TILLEY Trench respectively.

The Observation Post withdrawn to BETTY Trench must not be stationed further east than T.D.a.6.9. and the Observation section withdrawn into VESTA TILLEY must not be further east than T.d.d.7.5.

Battalion Headquarters will be informed when the sections have been withdrawn.

All troops in BETTY and VESTA TILLEY Communication trench will wear Box Respirators from Zero minus two minutes until orders for their removal are given by an Officer. This order should not be given until Zero plus 30 minutes, and then only if the trench system is reported clear of Gas.

O.C. "B" and "D" Companies will report when their Observation Sections have Re-occupied their former positions.

6. The Battalion Gas N.C.O. with six other ranks, to be detailed by O.C. "A" Company, will proceed at Zero plus 10 minutes with three fans to clear the following portion of our Line:- "BETTY - BILLY BURKE - TOLEDO - VESTA TILLEY - .

The Gas N.C.O. will report all clear to an Officer of "D" Company at junction of VESTA TILLEY and TEDDY GERRARD, and to an Officer of "B" Company at junction of BETTY and ACTRESS.

The Party to be supplied from "A" Company will report to the Gas N.C.O. at 11 p.m. on the night 5/6th July at junction of KEEMS and BETTY.

The Gas N.C.O. will clear the above mentioned trenches beginning at junction of BETTY and ACTRESS, and ending at junction of VESTA TILLEY and TEDDY GERRARD.

The Gas Curtains will be drawn in all dug-outs in the BLUE LINE from Zero minus two minutes until orders for their removal are given by an Officer.

O.Cs. "D", "C", "A" and "B" Companies will see this order carried out, and will arrange that their Company Gas N.C.Os. inspect the BLUE LINE for traces of Gas and report all clear to them before the order to raise Gas Curtains is given. All clear report will be forwarded immediately to Battalion Headquarters by the code word "TALK".

The presence of Gas will be reported by the code word "NASTY".

7. A special Fuller 'phone with Station will be established by the Brigade at the Test Box at the junction of DORIS and KEEMS. Lieut. J.W.Parr and two battalion runners will be stationed at this Test Box from 12.30 p.m. until the operation is complete.

Lieut. Parr will receive from Brigade Signaller in charge a copy of all R.E. communications sent through. He will send one copy by wire direct to Brigade, repeating same to Battalion Headquarters. A code has been issued separately to Lieut. Parr for his use, and he must do everything possible to obtain reports of the progress of the operation.

ORDER No 13 (contd.).

8. The decision will be made by higher Authority at 1 p.m. on 5th July or succeeding days as to whether the operation shall take place, and all concerned shall be notified as early as possible. The code used will be:-
    The Operation will take place to-night.   JAPAN.
    Operation postponed.   SPAIN.
    Cancel Operation previously ordered.   RUSSIA.

9. Zero will be at 12.30 a.m. or as soon after as the trucks are reported to be in position.

10. Watches will be synchronized at 7.30 p.m.. For this purpose the Signalling Officer will send a watch to each Company at that hour.

                                                  Lieut.,
4th July, 1916.   Adjutant, 6th H.L.I.

No 1 Copy.	O.C. "A" Company.
2	" "B" "
3	" "C" "
4	" "D" "
5	Lieut. J.R.Parr.
6	Signalling Officer.
7	O.i/c Lewis Gun Section.
8	Battalion Gas N.C.O.
9	Adjutant.
10	War Diary.
11	War Diary.
12	File.

5th H.L.I.
Appendix 3
Copy No 11

ORDER No 15.
15th July, 1918.

Reference MARCEUIL 1/20000.

1. **INFORMATION.** The 155th Brigade will relieve the 157th Brigade in the Left Section of the Divisional Front on 17th July, 1918.

2. **INTENTION.** The 5th R.S.F. will relieve this Battalion on 17th July, 1918, and the Battalion after relief will proceed to LANCASTER and FRASER Camps, near MONT St. ELOI.

3. **ORDERS TO TROOPS.** (1) Relief of Companies.

   "A" Coy. 5th R.S.F. will relieve "D" Coy. 5th H.L.I.
   "C" " " " " " "C" " " "
   "D" " " " " " "A" " " "
   "B" " " " " " "B" " " "

   (2) Guides. O.C. Companies will detail one Officer per Company and one guide per platoon; Headquarters one N.C.O. and two guides. These guides will be marched under their Officer and be at the foot of HUMBER Trench at 10.30 a.m.

   (3) The order of March of the Companies of the 5th R.S.F. will be "B", "D", "C", "A", "H.Q."

   (4) The guides will take the following routes:-

   "B" Coy. 5th R.S.F., RED TRAIL - BRIDGE at T.13.c.15.15. - Headquarters - BOIS DE LA CHAUDIERE - BLUENOSE - YARMOUTH.
   "D" Coy., 5th R.S.F. same route as far as Headquarters then through Tunnel and by HAYTER.
   "C" Coy. 5th R.S.F. RED TRAIL to PEGGY. Two platoons for BLACK LINE by GERTIE; two platoons for BLUE LINE by PEGGY.
   "A" Coy. 5th R.S.F. same route as for "C" Coy. 5th R.S.F.
   The Scout Officer will detail two scouts to be at the barrier at 10 a.m. to direct the 5th R.S.F. to the HUMBER TRACK. These guides will move to the new Camp with Hdqrs Coy.

   (5) Handing over. All trench stores will be handed over to relieving unit and receipts obtained.
   Companies will hand over 175 filled Magazines and 88 Tin Cases each. The L.G.O. will arrange to hand over the Battn. Reserve at Hdqrs, viz., 400 Magazines and 80 Tin Cases and one Anti-Aircraft Mount-ing. Eight Magazines will be carried by each team. All drums and ammunition must be thoroughly clean.
   Companies will hand over the following number of dixies:-

   "A" Coy. 7   "B" Coy. 6
   "C" " 7   "D" " 7
   H.Q. Coy. 8

   (6) Relief Complete will be wired to Battalion Headquarters by priority wire. Code Word "JOHN"

   (7) Marching Out. On relief Companies will proceed independently to the barrier on the NEUVILLE St VAAST Road using the same routes as their relieving Companies respectively. They will move in parties of two sections at 100 yards distance.

   (8) Embussing. The busses which bring up the 5th R.S.F. will take this Battalion to new Camps. The 157th Brigade Embussing Officers are Lieut. J.M.Stewart and LIEUT. M.D. Nicolson. 2/Lieut. R. Park, "D" Coy., is appointed Embussing Officer for the Battalion and will report to the Brigade Officers at the Barrier at 12 noon. Each bus will carry one platoon or as ordered by the Embussing Officer.
   Each party will be drawn up on the right side of the

Orders No 13 (contd).

9. In the event of an Alarm or at Attack during the relief troops will halt and man the nearest defences, reporting their position at once to Brigade Headquarters. Commanding Officer will remain with the relieving C.O. and await orders from Bge

10. Hostile Aircraft. In the event of the approach of hostile aircraft, parties will clear off the road and remain still until the danger is past.

11. Dress. Fighting order with greatcoat rolled on belt.

12. Advance party from 5th R.S.F. An Advance party consisting of one Officer and one N.C.O. per Coy and Hdqrs will arrive on the morning of 16th instant to take over trench stores. The Scout Officer will detail a guide to meet this party at the foot of HUMBER Trench at 10.30 a.m. He will guide them to Bn. Hdqrs. where they will be met by guides which will be detailed by Coys to take them to the Coys they are taking over from.

13. The Sigs Sergt will hand over over Signalling Equipment, except Regtl. property, and take a receipt. He will also see that the runners at Hdqrs and at Relay posts Nos 1 & 2 are relieved.

14. Advance Baggage. O.C. Coys will arrange to send down all surplus baggage and stores by the train returning from VICTORIA Dump on the night of 16th inst. They will arrange to load this and send down one batman per Coy in charge. The Transport Officer will arrange to carry this baggage from ZIVY Dump to the new Camp.

15. The four pioneers at present with the Battn will proceed to ZIVY Dump with the returning train on the night of 16th inst. and report to the Acting Adjutant for work on the new Camp before the arrival of the Battn.

                                                Thegate Lieut.,
                                            A/Adjt., 5th H. L. I.

Copy No		
1	O.C.	"A" Coy,
2	"	"B" "
3	"	"C" "
4	"	"D" "
5	"	5th R.S.F.
6	O.i/c	Lewis Guns.
7	"	Scouts.
8	T.O.	
9	Q.M.	
10	A/Adjt.,	
11	War Diary.	
12	War Diary.	

5th E. L. I. Appendix No 4.   Copy No 11

ADMINISTRATIVE INSTRUCTIONS TO CAMP No 13.

15th July, 1918

1. **Transport.** The Transport will remain in its present site.

2. **Supplies.** Rations for 18th will be drawn as at present from LEARMAY SIDING and sent to LANCASTER and FRAZER Camps. Rations for consumption on 19th will be drawn from BLACKPOOL Siding. The Q.M. will include in his ration strength for the 18th the Nucleus and reinf crements at present at VILLERS.

3. **Water.** Water is led into the Camps. Strict supervision will be exercised to prevent wastage.

4. **Billet Improvements.** The 5th R.S.F. will hand over their Scheme of Work for the billet sanitation and minor improvements, and a Schedule of the work in progress.

5. **Duties.** The battn. will supply the Brigade duties on the 20th instant. The Guards and picquets to be provided are detailed in 157th Bdge Administration Instruction No 108.

6. Duties to be furnished by Battalion.

Duty.	Strength.	Location.	Time to report.
(1) Prisoners of War Cage.	1 Off, 1 N.C.O. and 12 men.	A.6.c.5.7.	See A.I. No A.Y.9 of 25/5/18 and amendment "A" Summary No 4 of 11/6/18.

The names of the Officer, N.C.O. and Men detailed for the above will be sent direct to the A.P.M.

(2) Water Picquet	1 man.	F.6.a.5.9.	Drinking.
		F.4.b.5.1.	Horses.
	1 man.	F.9.d.5.1.	"
		F.9.d.4.5.	Drinking.
	1 man.	F.9.c.9.6.	"
		F.9.c.9.5.	Horses.
	1 man.	F.11.b.1.2.	"
		F.11.b.C.5.	"
	1 man.	F.10.d.1.5.	Tank.
		F.10.d.1.6.	Horses.

7. O.i/c Nucleus at VILLERS will move to the new Camp on the morning of 17th inst. He will arrange with the A/Adjt. as to accommodation. Reinforcements will be given quarters to themselves until they are allotted to Coys.

8. The Q.M. will remain at the Transport Lines and the A/Q.M. will be with the Battn at the New Camp.

9. **Messing.** The Coys in Lancaster Camp and the two Coys and H.Q. in FRAZER Camp will mess in the Dining Huts provided. Separate instructions are being issued.
Platoons will be marched to the dining huts.

10. **Discipline.** N.C.Os and men are forbidden to leave the Divisional Area. ECOIVRES and other villages in the 51st Divl. Area south of and east and west line through cross roads F.14.b.10.0. are strictly out of bounds for all troops of the Bge.

11. **Bounds.** The bounds for the Bge are marked by 52nd Divl boards at the following points:-
F.10.a.1.7.   M.14.a.8.7
F.13.b.6.6.   F.13.c.9.0.
F.7.d.6.2.

No N.C.O. or man is allowed outside these areas except in possession of a pass signed by the Commanding Officer and bearing the Office stamp.

Administrative Instructions (contd).

Battalion bounds will be marked by notice boards. No man will leave the area of the three Camps at ANZAC or ELGI without a belt.

12. The Baths at BERTHONVAL FARM have been allotted to the Battn. from 8 a.m. to 12 noon and 2 p.m. to 6 p.m. on 16th inst. Their capacity is 60 men each half hour. The following is the roster arranged for Coys.

```
"A" Coy      9 a.m.    to    10 a.m.
"B"  "      10   "     "     11.30 a.m.
"C"  "      11.30 a.m.        12 noon.
             1 p.m.           2 p.m.
"D"          2 p.m.           3.30 p.m.
"H.Q."       3.30 p.m.        6 p.m.
```

O.C. Coys will make their own arrangements for having their men bathed within the allotted hours.
Dress Clean fatigue with puttees. Towel and soap will be carried.

13. Area Stores at Lancaster and Fraser Camps. The A/Adjt. will arrange for an Officer at the Nucleus to take over these Stores at 8.30 a.m. on 17th instant.

14. Exchanged Lewis Gun Magazines, Tin Boxes, etc. The L.G. N.C.O. will take over from the 5th R.S.F. at OTTAWA Camp the Magazines, etc., exchanged, viz.,
    1164 Magazines, 136 Tin Cases, and
    1 Anti-Aircraft Mounting.
The Transport Officer will arrange to have these conveyed to the new Camp on 17th instant.

15. Arrival at Camp. O.i/c Nucleus will arrange with the A/Adjt. for the coys being met on arrival at Camp and shown to their respective quarters.

16. The following Technical Stores will be withdrawn into Regmtl. Stores on the day of arrival in Camp:-
    Hedging Gloves.   Small Periscopes.
    Runners Badges.   Wire Cutters.
    Grenade Belt Carriers.   Grenade Buckets.

17. Regimental Shops. Will open at FRASER Camp at 12 noon on 17th inst. Allocation to Coys is as follows:-

	Tailors.	Cobblers.	Barbers.
17th July.	"A"	"B"	"C"
18th	"D"	"H.Q."	"A"
19th	"B"	"C"	"D"
20th	"H.Q."	"A"	"B"
21st	"C"	"D"	"H.Q."
22nd	"A"	"B"	"C"
23rd	"D"	"H.Q."	"A"
24th	"B"	"C"	"D"
25th	"H.Q."	"A"	"B"

Shepate Lieut.,
A/Adjt., 5th H.L.I.

```
Copy No 1  O.C. "A" Coy.
       2   "    "B" "
       3   "    "C" "
       4   "    "D" "
       5  O.i/c Nucleus.
       6   "    Lewis Guns.
       7   "    Scouts.
       8  T.O.
       9  Q.M.
      10  A/Adjt.
      11  War Diary.
      12  War Diary.
```

Appendix No. 5.

5th H.L.I.　　　　　　　　　Copy No 12

ORDER No 14.　　　　　　　24th July, 1918.

Reference Maps LENS 11.　} 1/100000.
　　　　　　　　HAZEBROUCK }

1. From 12 noon on 23rd July, 1918, the 52nd Division is in G.H.Q. Reserve. The 157th Brigade will be ready to move by Bus or Tactical Train at six hours notice after 12 noon 23rd July, 1918.

2. (a) Entraining Station, if moving by Tactical Train, will be PERNES. Transport, with the exception of the four Lewis Gun Limbers, Field Kitchens, Officers' Chargers and Pack Animals will proceed by road. The Lewis Gun Limbers, etc., will be taken in an Omnibus Train, for which separate Orders will be issued.

　　(b) Move by bus. The head of the Embussing Point is at Y in CHAUCY La TOUR. Lewis Guns will be carried, together with 24 filled Lewis Gun drums per gun. One day's ration will be carried on the men. A bus will take one Officer and 25 Other Ranks; a lorry will take one Officer and 20 Other Ranks.
　　　On Orders being issued to prepare to move, O.C. Companies will send an Officer immediately to Battalion Headquarters to receive Orders.

3. Orders will be issued later as regards dress and equipment.

4. O.C. "B" Company will detail one platoon to load the S.A.A., Tools and Lewis Gun Magazines Limbers. This party will be told off on receipt of these Orders, and No. of platoon intimated to Hdqrs. O.C. "D" Company will also detail one platoon for loading Officers' baggage.
　　Companies will each load their own Lewis Gun Limbers.

5. Dump. It is possible that a dump will require to be formed in the present battalion area. Orders will be issued with regard to this.

6. Rations. The Quartermaster will arrange that all rations are issued immediately on receipt of Orders to move. The Field Kitchens will be completed and ready to pull out at the same time as the limbers are loaded.

7. Transport. The Transport Officer will arrange to send his teams and Pack Animals complete to Q.M. Stores, and will report to Hdqrs. when ready to move.

8. Nucleus. It is possible that the Training Nucleus may be left behind if the Battalion moves. O.C. Companies will arrange to have prepared lists of their men whom they propose to leave behind to form a Nucleus. Men on Leave and at Courses will count as Nucleus.

9. O.C. "B" Company will detail an Officer to supervise the entraining or embussing. This Officer will report to Headquarters

on the Order being received to move.

10. Reports. Companies will report when they are ready to move.

11. The order of embussing or entraining will be:-

    Headquarters Company.
    "A" Company.
    "B"   "
    "C"   "
    "D"   "

Companies before moving off will have their men told off in bus loads, and will report the figures to Headquarters.

                                                 Lieut.,
                                 A/Adjt., 5th Bn. R. I. R.

        No 1 O.C. "A" Coy.
            2 "   "B" "
            3 "   "C" "
            4 "   "D" "
            5 "   O.i/c Transport.
            6 "   "   Sigs.
            7 "   "   Scouts, L.Gs.
            8 Quartermaster.
            9 Adjutant.
           10 2nd in Command.
           11 War Diary.
           12 "   "

5th BATTN. H.L.I.

REFERENCE: ORDER No. 14.

It is probable that if an order to move is received it will be between the hours of midnight and 8 a.m.

The difficulty to get all ranks awakened when scattered in billets is realised, and to obviate this difficulty the following procedure will be adopted:-

The Signaller on duty, when he receives the wire ordering the move, will at once despatch same to the Adjutant and send to the Runners' Hut to awaken the Runners. There are 15 Runners in the Hut, and they will be used as follows:-

    2 to report to the Adjutant.
    1 to awake each Officer commanding a Coy.
    1 " " the Transport Officer.
    1 " " " Regimental Sergeant Major.
    1 " " each Coy. Hut.
    1 " " Headquarters Huts.
    1 " " Quartermaster's Stores.
    1 " " Orderly Room and Canteen Hut.

These Orderlies will be detailed by name by the N.C.O. I/C Signallers. When called they will not wait to put on equipment, but, after putting on their boots, will double out and carry out their duties, and when completed will report at Orderly Room for further orders.

The Orderly Officer sleeping in the Orderly Room will be responsible that these orders are carried out. The Signaller on duty will be instructed to awaken him immediately he receives a wire for the Battalion to move.

24th July, 1918.

                                                Lieut.,
                                               Adjutant.

8th BATTN. H.L.I.

Reference: Order No. 14, Para. 3.

DRESS.

For action, the Pack will be carried, and will contain:-

Balmoral, Rations, Mess Tin, Knife, Fork and Spoon, Razor, Soap, Towel, Spare Socks, 1 Spare Shirt, Cardigan, Housewife, Cap Comforter, Oil Tin and Flannellette, and Haversack empty. The Waterproof Sheet will be carried folded under the flap of the Pack.

For the Move, Greatcoats will be carried in the Pack. These will be dumped on arrival.

[signature] Lieut.,
Adjutant.

4th July, 1918.

SECRET.   Appendix N°6   5th H. L. I.   Copy No 12

ORDER No.15.

I. **INFORMATION.** The 17th Corps will relieve the Canadian Corps in the ARRAS Sector of the Line. Infantry reliefs will probably commence on night 31st July - 1st August.

    (2) The 52nd Division will occupy the Left Sub Sector of the Corps Front with three Brigades in the Line.

    (3) The 157th Brigade Group will move to-morrow, 30th instant, by road to billets in BARLIN.

II. **INTENTION.** The Battalion will move to BARLIN to-morrow.

III. **ORDERS TO TROOPS.** 1. Companies will be clear of huts by 8 a.m. and will parade on Company Parade Grounds ready to move 8.30 a.m.

    The order of March will be Hdqrs Coy., "A" "B" "C" "D" Transport.

    The head of the column will pass the top entrance to CHATEAU Grounds at 8.45 a.m.

    The route will be LOZINGHEM - MARLES LES MINES - CAMBLAIN CHATELAIN - HOUDAIN.

    Halts - 10 minutes halt will take place at 10 minutes to each clock hour.

    (2) All baggage will be stacked ready to load at Q.M. Dump by 7 a.m. to-morrow.

    "C" Company will supply a loading party of two sections to report to Q.M. at 7 a.m.

    (3) **TRANSPORT.** Transport will accompany the Battalion and will be loaded by 8 a.m.

    S.A.A., Lewis Gun and Tool Limbers will be loaded to-night. In addition to 1st Line Transport and Baggage Wagons, two motor lorries will be at the disposal of the battalion. If necessary these lorries are available for a second run. Time at which lorries will report will be notified later.

    (4) **DRESS & EQUIPMENT.** Fighting Order will be worn. The haversack will contain:- Cardigan, Towel and Soap, Shaving kit, Socks, Cap Comforter, unconsumed portion of day's rations. The Iron Rations will be carried in Mess Tin slung on haversack. Waterproof sheet under flap of haversack. Steel Helmet will be carried on back of haversack.

    Packs will be stacked beside Q.M. Stores in Company Dumps by 7 a.m. The Q.M. will select dumps and see that these are clearly marked. Each Company will detail small loading party to load its own packs.

    (5) **ROUTINE.** To-morrow, 30th instant:-

        Reveille 5.30 a.m.
        Sick Parade 6 a.m.
        Breakfast 6.30 a.m.

    Dinners will be issued on arrival in New Camp.

    (6) **STATE.** A Marching out State will be rendered before Coys. move off.

    (7) **SUPPLIES.** Rations for the Brigade Group for the 31st will be delivered direct to units in their new area by train wagons. Location of Railhead and Refilling Point will be notified later.

over/

(2)

8. **WATER.** Water bottles will be filled from the carts to-morrow as under:-

       "A"   5.45 a.m.
       "B"   6.00 a.m.
       "C"   6.15 a.m.
       "D"   7.00 a.m.
      H.Q.   7.15 a.m.

                                         Lieut.,
                              A/Adjt., 5th H. L. I.

29th July, 1918.

                Copy No 1   O.C. "A" Coy.
                        2   "   "B" "
                        3   "   "C" "
                        4   "   "D" "
                        5   O.i/c H.Q. "
                        6   Transport Officer.
                        7   Quartermaster.
                        8   2nd in Command.
                        9   A/Adjutant.
                     10   R.S.M.
                     11)   War Diary.
                     12)

5th H.L.I.

War Diary, Volume 39.
August, 1918.

OEF-
39/1.
5th H.L.I.
157/5~

Army Form C. 2118.

WAR DIARY
or
INTELLIGENCE SUMMARY
(Erase heading not required.)

Instructions regarding War Diaries and Intelligence Summaries are contained in F. S. Regs., Part II. and the Staff Manual respectively. Title Pages will be prepared in manuscript.

Place	Date	Hour	Summary of Events and Information	Remarks and references to Appendices
ECURIE WOOD	1/8/16		Received orders for Brigade to leave our Camp at ECURIE WOOD CAMP within the BROWN LINE so to be on within ROCLINCOURT. Took over BROWN LINE with three Coys. A Coy. left at ECURIE WOOD CAMP. Relief conducted by Coys. and completed by 1700. A Coy. Subsequently moved up by Brigade order to BRIERLY TRENCH & thence moved to ECURIE. BHs.	MARŒUIL 2.0000
	2/8/16		Day showery. Hostile shells known on left & Right area within time day having line had over line being duckboards regiment. Considerable congestion on right which EMBANKMENT kept & other masked BHs.	
	3/8/16		Day showery, trenches wet to duckboards very muddy. Enemy reported several Pats of BROWN LINE and EMBANKMENT. A few 4.5 shells at rifle 400 yd. station, other distinctly fell Georgyria. BHs.	
	4/8/16		Lt-Col. Neilson returned from leave at 1st Army & resumed command. Day & night quiet, still showery. Warned that Batts will relieve 8th HLI in Right Subsection on 7th. Made preliminary arrangements. Went round line in afternoon. Day quiet. Nightfire two guns fell.	
	5/8/16		At 0500 Enemy shelled Embankment front-work & both ridges with 5.9" no damage. Day showery. Arranged with OC 6th HLI. details of relief. Went round line. Day & night quiet.	
	6/8/16		At Cornichet to Hospital sick.	
	7/8/16		Relieved 6 & 8 HLI in Right Subsection of OPPY SECTION (new No.13). Relief complete 1830.	Appendix No 1

WAR DIARY / INTELLIGENCE SUMMARY

Army Form C. 2118.

30/2. 5th H.L.I.

Place	Date	Hour	Summary of Events and Information	Remarks and references to Appendices
	7/9/18		Capt NEIR left to become Assistant Town Major ARRAS. Issued orders (No.17) Appendix 2 with regard to Gas teams which were discharged in our area. So soon as enemy is favourable Defensive Patrol. B Coy. Lt SHEDDEN. Night guard. B Coy.	MORNING 1.2.0.000 ROUTINE ORDNC. 37. N.W.1 OPPY SH. NW 2 1/10,000 Apdx 2. "3
	8/9/18		2nd Lieut - Ms CUMMING returned from leave & resumed duties as I.O. Appointed Adjutant of Coy (Order No. 18) Appendix 3. Night guard. Defensive Patrol B Coy. Lt NICHOLSON." A Coy at RMCK. Test S.O.S. at 9.30 P.M. fell.	
	9/9/18		Capt NICKER took over command of B Coy from Capt CURRIE to proceed. Lt FRASER to home leave. Went to Coy & agreed with Capt. FYFE regarding laying out of Coy's defences locality. 1. Coy. 5th HLI placed at my disposal for work on the 2 defended localities. Arranged with Engineers with regard to starting on "Baby Elephants" in POST LINE. Defensive Patrols. D & B Coys. Night guard. fell.	
	10/9/18		Fine weather. Day quiet. Major BRAND rather officious. Court of enquiry meeting in accordance with 32nd Division memo. that all officers should be on the trench duties. There was an attack 8305. Heavy enemy shelling on our right. Our barrage put down. S.O.S. from Rt. Brigade at 0340. Firing died down shortly after 0400. Noticeable. Enemy distinct not pattern was uncomfortable that enemy hustled off hole of 57 Kr Brigade on our right fell.	

WAR DIARY or INTELLIGENCE SUMMARY

Army Form C. 2118.

39/3

3rd W.F. 1

Place	Date	Hour	Summary of Events and Information	Remarks and references to Appendices
Lire	11/9/18		Ordered by B.H.Commander to reduce the number of platoons holding Row TRENCH from 3 to 2. So not like the Machine Gun Post Stand games effects (Order No 19 appendix 4). Day fine & quiet. Capt L H WATSON went down to machine gun course from Capt C ARRIS who there up command of B Coy. Capt MORRISON resumes command of D Coy from Lieut Agnew. Watson to return. Permitted where offensive patrols. A Coy (Lt ROGERS) - B Coy Lt HUDSON - no enemy seen. Night quiet. Still	ROCLINCOURT 5·8 M.W.1 0.P.Y. 3rd W.F. W.2 1/25/1910
	12/9/18		Day fine - quiet. Daylight patrol return afternoon. Got within 250x of enemy M/guns. Patrol B Coy Lt ROBERTSON reconnoitred enemy wire support of DUKE ST. Enemy working party found moving. Night quiet. Prepared scheme for raid. Still.	
	13/9/18		Showery. Warm. Received warning order that Br Br would relieve our division commencing night 14/15. A Coy relieved C Coy in front zone. Offensive Patrol B Coy (Lt SHEDDEN) Nil	
	14/9/18		Hot. Quiet. Went to lecture & demonstration by I.C.T. (Lt Col MAXSE). Enemy shelled support of M/G Warwick Post held by D Coy with mountain gun. No casualties until morning when about 15 men affected. All rescue shell holes filled in. Warned into C/field. 1 OR wounded at Raton thrown by shell fired. Warned that 2 Br Div wounded relieve us in place of 61st Brit - Still.	
	15/9/18		OC. 2nd Northamptons arrived to arrange details of relief on night 16/17. Capt M. ROSS R.A.M.C. (J.C.) arrived as M.O. to relieve Capt MORTON returned to ROUEN for two months rest. Day & night quiet. Still.	

WAR DIARY
or
INTELLIGENCE SUMMARY

Army Form C. 2118.

5th H.L.I.   39/4

Place	Date	Hour	Summary of Events and Information	Remarks and references to Appendices
Arras	14/9/18		Fine. Warm. Received warning that Bath. would on relief move to West Camp ROCLINCOURT + on 17 7 by train to CHATEAU-de-la HAIE area. Relieved by 2nd Northamptons (order No 20 Appendix A). Relief complete 9.30 P.M. Bath. marched back to Rockincourt, all Coys in by 11 P.M.	ROCKINCOURT ODSX ¼000 appendix A 5 " " 6
CHATEAU DE LA HAIE	17/9/18		Received orders at 9 A.M. to march to CHATEAU de la HAIE area. Starting at 2 P.M. (order No 21, appx B) Arrived in Camp at 5.15 P.M. after hard march owing to wind & dust. New Camp floor. Collected all surplus baggage into Regimental dump. Fell	LENS ¼000 appendix B
"	18/9/18		Sent Regimental dump to AUBIGNY. Day first. Coys training. CO's conference at 10 a.m. - expounded of intended attack by XVII Corps on Enemy positions South of River SCARPE East of ARRAS. Allotted Platn. to each battalion. Went with Brigade Commander to reconnoitre ground. Enemy bombed vicinity of camp at night no damage. New Thorburn A.T.M. arrived being attached for 1 month. Fell	
"	19/9/18 20/9/18		Day Drill. Coys platoon training. Fell " " " " Barking. at 6 P.M. warned to send billeting party to AGNEZ LES DUISANS + take early tomorrow by motor march in evening. Proceeded 10.15 A.M. (order No 22 appx F) arriving at Y huts at 2.15 next. Bath. marched well. Fell	
AGNEZ LES DUISANS	21/9/18		Fine warmer. Inspected Church whole. Accommodation quite good. Many men with blistered feet.	appx 7.
BEAUCOURT "	22/9/18		Spent day at AGNEZ LES DUISANS, moved at 12.15 P.M. to BEAUCOURT. BMS.	

Army Form C. 2118.

WAR DIARY
or
INTELLIGENCE SUMMARY.   5R H.L.I.

(Erase heading not required.)

Place	Date	Hour	Summary of Events and Information	Remarks and references to Appendices
BEWACOURT	23/8/18		Arrived at 4.30 a.m. rested in a field. Moved at 5 p.m. by motor lorry to position N.E. of FICHEUX in S.2.a. Men rested in old trenches. DWS	Map: FRANCE 51 B.S.W. 1/20,000
	24/8/18		At 2am received orders for attack to be made by Brigade this morning. The Brigade is to pass through the 156 Brigade, their line running from T.2.c.50 to T.1.a.8.8, attacking Eastwards and finally assaulting and consolidating the portion of the HINDENBURG LINE (front and support system) between T.5.a and M.34.d. 5th and 6th H.L.I. to deliver the attack, 5th on the Left, 6th on the Right, 7th H.L.I. in Reserve. At 4.45 AM the battalion moved in artillery formation ('A' and 'D' Coys forming 1st Line, 'B' & 'C' Coys the 2nd) to position of assembly (Railway embankment in S.3). At 5.30 AM continued advance. Our own bombardment opened at 7AM and the battalion came under enemy shell-fire. The river COJEUL was crossed in T.2.c. On crossing the sunken road in T.3.c. Coys extended. Headquarters was established at T.3. Central at 7.45 AM. By this time under Rifle and M.G. fire and moderate enemy H.E. fire. About 8.30 AM Col NEILSON was severely wounded and Capt FYFE took command until Capt PARR could be informed. The Advance continued to about 300 yards of the wire in front of our first objective,	Appendix No. 8

Army Form C. 2118.

WAR DIARY
INTELLIGENCE SUMMARY. 5th H.L.I.
(Erase heading not required.)

39/6

Place	Date	Hour	Summary of Events and Information	Remarks and references to Appendices
			which ran from T.4.9.8. to M.34.d.0.2., without check. There it was held up by our own barrage which was falling in some cases behind our front line. This was about 9 A.M. Some dragging fire was put over at this time by the enemy. At 9.15AM the Right Coy. "A", was withdrawn about 50 yards to clear our barrage, at the same time small parties of the enemy were seen withdrawing from his front line. The line at this moment ran from T.4.d.8.9. to T.4.d.5.6. with supporting Coy. echeloned to left rear at T.4.a. There was a gap on our left in M.32.b., a distance of about 1500 yards which was maintained with 6th H.L.I. on the Right. At 10 A.M. the barrage was continuing to fall in front of and behind our front line. It was entirely from our Heavy Artillery. Capt. FYFE consulted O.C. 6th H.L.I. (Col. ANDERSON) as to the advisability of pushing on through our barrage. It was decided to remain in present position. Five runners were sent to Brigade asking for the barrage to be lifted at 10.30 AM. Capt. PARR, being senior, took over command from Capt. FYFE. At 11.15 AM the barrage stopped and at 11.30 AM 2 Platoons "A" Coy. and 2 Platoons "B" Coy., under Capt. L.H. WATSON,	

WAR DIARY or INTELLIGENCE SUMMARY.

5th H.L.I.

Army Form C. 2118.

Place	Date	Hour	Summary of Events and Information	Remarks and references to Appendices
	39/7		advanced on HINDENBURG line. The wire was no visible from headquarters and the Matoons could be seen trying to get through. It was exceptionally thick and strong and the Platoons were under heavy T.M. and M.G. fire. One T.M. was located and a request to Brigade to have guns turned on was sent. This was not complied with. Casualties among the assaulting Platoons were heavy 2/Lieut Turner being killed and Lieut. BARR wounded. At 12.15 P.M. the assaulting Platoons being unable to get through the wire withdrew to old line to allow T.M.s to be neutralised. At 1.45 P.M. the B.Q.C. came to Headquarters and an assault with 2/4 H.L.I. was arranged to follow a 15 minutes' bombardment on HINDENBURG front and support lines, Zero for assault being fixed at 3.45 P.M. No bombardment took place until 3.43 P.M. At 3.46 P.M. 6th H.L.I. moved no they were directing 5th conformed. Formation of Coys. was S as at the beginning of the advance. The wire was again impeded the advance. That by 5 P.M. the wire was penetrated. It was about 30 yards in front of front line. At 5.15 P.M. advance held up between wire and front line by	

WAR DIARY

INTELLIGENCE SUMMARY

Army Form C. 2118

5th H.L.I.

29/8

Place	Date	Hour	Summary of Events and Information	Remarks and references to Appendices
			M.G. and T.M. firing from left flank. A Platoon of 'C' Coy. was sent up to prolong left flank; it took up reserve S.A.A. at 5.30 P.M. Heavy bombardment by enemy at 5.45 P.M. An assault had been made and a footing obtained on our front objective at 6 P.M. By this time had to be evacuated; casualties had been heavy. There was no outpost on left flank and troops had been fallen back with the 6th H.L.I. on the right and a counter attack from the left had commenced. Two prisoners were brought back. A new line was formed; by 7 P.M. the line was organised as before the assault and at 8 P.M. was withdrawn 200 yards to conform with troops on our right and a Coy. of 7th H.L.I. placed under our orders to assist in holding line. At this time only touch with 6th H.L.I. was by patrol and the 6th H.L.I. sent a Platoon to fill the gap. The Battalion spent the night in this position. Between 8 P.M. and 9.30 P.M. the enemy directed a very heavy bombardment on the area occupied by us. After that the night was fairly quiet. There was no hostile activity on the part of the enemy, our defensive patrols seeing nothing. Our casualties were:- Killed Officers: 2/Lieut E.D.TURNER. Wounded:	

1875 Wt. W593/826 1,000,000 4/15 J.B.C. & A. A.D.S.S./Forms/C. 2118.

Army Form C. 2118.

WAR DIARY
—or—
INTELLIGENCE SUMMARY.   5th H.L.I.
(Erase heading not required.)

Instructions regarding War Diaries and Intelligence Summaries are contained in F. S. Regs., Part II. and the Staff Manual respectively. Title pages will be prepared in manuscript.

Place	Date	Hour	Summary of Events and Information	Remarks and references to Appendices
			Capt. L.H.WATSON. 2/Lieut. E.T.WILLIAMSON. 2/Lieut. C.M.SANDERSON. Lieut. J. GIRVAN. Lieut. G.S. BARR. Lieut-Colonel J.B.NEILSON died of wounds: Lieut. A.H.MALCOLM promoted of San:- 2/Lieut J.McKIE. Missing: Capt. R.M.MILLER, Lieut. J.W. PARR. Other Ranks:- Killed 13, Wounded 162, Missing and unaccounted for 80; Total Other Ranks 255.	
	25/9/18		At 4 A.M. heavy bombardment by enemy. Headquarters forced to move to another shell-hole. Major 'BRAND' from nucleus took over command at 5.30 A.M. Battalion dispositions no alteration on night mainly in shell-holes. Intermittent shelling and T.M. fire all day and movement enforced to hostile M.G. fire. Circling enemy planes over at various times of the day. At 8.30 P.M. under orders from B.G.C. lines was withdrawn from Battalion 5th H.L.I. less 'A' and 'B' Coys, moving into Brigade Reserve in HENIN - ST. LEGER Road in T.3.c., the 6th and 7th H.L.I. holding	

WAR DIARY
INTELLIGENCE SUMMARY 5th H.L.I.

Army Form C. 2118

Place	Date	Hour	Summary of Events and Information	Remarks and references to Appendices
39/10			the HENIN - CROISILLES Road in T.3.b. 'A' and 'B' Coys, under Capt. FYFE, were sent to hold HENIN HILL in T.4.d. and T.5.c. HENIN HILL was patrolled throughout the night. Casualties :- Other Ranks	
	26/8/18		Killed 1, wounded 8. At 3 AM 'A' and 'B' Coys were withdrawn from HENIN HILL and rejoined Battalion in Road. The day was quiet, very few shells falling near the road. Lieut CUMMING reconnoitred HENIN HILL and reported HINDENBURG line opposite and FOOLEY TRENCH held by enemy, as he had been under T.M. and M.G. fire from them during the day. The 153 Brigade were working down HINDENBURG line. A patrol of one Platoon sent out to relieve Lieut. CUMMING returned all gassed, but not seriously. Casualties :- Other Ranks gassed, 3; Capt M.W. PARR to hospital, sick.	
	27/8/18		At 4 AM received Warning Order that Brigade would attack and to be ready to move at 8 AM. The general orders were to capture FONTAINE CROISILLES and continue advance S.E. and take RIENCOURT. 6th and 7th H.L.I. assaulting battalions, 5th H.L.I. Brigade Reserve. Inro Coys. 5th H.L.I. to mch wh FONTAINE	

WAR DIARY
INTELLIGENCE SUMMARY. 5th H.L.I.

39/11

Army Form C. 2118.

Place	Date	Hour	Summary of Events and Information	Remarks and references to Appendices
CROISILLES			Orders were given verbally to Coy Commanders. "B" and "C" Coys in front line, "A" and "D" Coys in second line. The two left Coys, "B" and "D" were detailed to mop up FONTAINE-CROISILLES. Assaulting battalions assembled along line of SUMMIT TRENCH from T.4.b.6.0 to junction with HINDENBURG Support line at N.35.c.3.4. 5th H.L.I. about one mile in rear. At 9.20 A.M. the advance commenced, at first under heavy M.G. fire which caused many casualties. After passing FARMERS' TRENCH in T.5.b. it died down, a large number of M.Gs. light and heavy having been captured. Enemy artillery very active throughout advance — practically all H.E. shell, causing remarkably few casualties for the number of shells fired coming down the HINDENBURG line. Headquarters took a strong direction and arrived in the outskirts of CHERISY, which was being very heavily shelled. The right flank of the Canadians was formed in O.32.d. They then moved through FONTAINE-CROISILLES which was found unoccupied, and rejoined the battalion in the CROISILLES-FONTAINE ROAD in U.7.C.9.9. By this time "C" and "B"	

WAR DIARY
INTELLIGENCE SUMMARY

Place: 5th H.L.I.
Date: 29/12

Coys. had been in action. They were following the 7th H.L.I. but had lost sight of them. They were advancing across the SENSEE RIVER in a S.E. direction. On the front beyond the CROISILLES FONTAINE ROAD a field gun was firing at them at point blank range. The rear side of the road was rushed but Capt. FYFE led the Coys through, and captured the gun, and found the C.T. running from the road held by the enemy. This was attacked and 5 M.Gs. captured. Subsequently a trench in front was attacked by advancing from shellhole to shellhole then Lieut. LEGATE led a frontal met with 4 men but was killed. The Coys then withdrew to the C.T. Casualties in this attack were very heavy. The position taken was to the left and still in rear of the 7th H.L.I. and this action must have removed a serious danger to the left flank of the 7th H.L.I. The advance had now stopped and I went up to the 6th + 7th H.L.I. Headquarters to find out the situation. Got in touch there by phone and reported position to B.G.C., in particular that we had been through FONTAINE CROISILLES which was found evacuated. Received orders to draw into position in

WAR DIARY
INTELLIGENCE SUMMARY

5th H.L.I.

39/13

Place: RIENCOURT

rear of 6th H.L.I. to cover them during advance on RIENCOURT. Advance was timed for 4 P.M., then 4.30 P.M., then postponed. Finally orders received that the advance would be against a limited objective but that also was cancelled and orders received that we would be relieved by 57th Division, 9th King's Liverpools and 4th South Lancs relieving Brigade. At 3.30 P.M. received an order to send 2 Coys to hold FONTAINE. 'A' and 'C' Coys were sent there under command of Acting R.S.M. Jones, only one Coy. Officer being left — Lieut. W.H. MILNE. King's Liverpools arrived about 11 P.M., but South Lancs were not seen. Spent the night in FONTAINE ROAD. During the advance a great amount of abandoned enemy material was found, including large numbers of Machine Guns (light and heavy) Trench Mortars, Rifles, Packs, 1 anti-tank rifle. In the Pill Box at U.8.c.9.9., where our Headquarters were, a large bundle of files dealing with Defence Schemes were found; these were forwarded to Brigade. Casualties: Officers: Killed Lieut. F. LEGATE. Wounded: Capt. T.A. FYFE, 2/Lieut. G.F.

WAR DIARY

INTELLIGENCE SUMMARY

Army Form C. 2118.

5th H.L.I.   39/14

Place	Date	Hour	Summary of Events and Information	Remarks and references to Appendices
			BRODIE, 2/Lieut. J.B. ROBERTSON. Other Ranks: Killed 4. Missing 6. Wounded 44. Total Casualties from operations from 24th to 28th August, 1918:- Officers: Killed 2, Died of Wounds 1, Missing 3, Wounded 9. Other Ranks: Killed 18, Died of Wounds 1, Wounded 1, Missing 9. Missing 59. Wounded 233. Wounded Gas 14. Total: Officers 15. Other Ranks 334. DWS	
	28/8/18		Moved from CROISILLES FONTAINE ROAD to MERCATEL at 7.30 AM, having been informed that the J. Lancs were in position. They had moved by a different route to the one indicated to our guide. Cookers met the Battalion on the way and a hot meal was served. Arrived MERCATEL 11.30 AM, and camped in Field rest. DWS	
MERCATEL	29/8/18		Day spent reorganising. DWS	
"	30/8/18		Draft of 1 Officer (2/Lt. W. BRYSON) and 76 O.R. arrived. Most have seen service in France before. Attended Conference by C.O.s at Bgde Hqrs. decided to reorganise Companys on basis of 4 Coys. each with 2 platoons. MAJOR TROMBURN Louis Brown. wrote and written posted to B. Coy. Matters returned including CAPT. MAIN. DWS	

Army Form C. 2118.

39/15.   5ᵗʰ H.L.I.

WAR DIARY
or
INTELLIGENCE SUMMARY.

(Erase heading not required.)

Place	Date	Hour	Summary of Events and Information	Remarks and references to Appendices
MERCATEL	31/8/18.		Inspected Companies. 2/Lt. PARK rejoined from Hospital. Submitted to Brigade the following recommendations for award for work done in the action from 24ᵗʰ to 27ᵗʰ August.	
			Capt. T. A. FYFE M.C. for D.S.O.	
			C/Sjt. L. H. WATSON " M.C.	
			266377 Sjt. T. LOGAN " D.C.M.	
			260307 Pt. G. CLARK	
			260153 Sjt. J. CAMPBELL	
			202105 Pt. C.P. STROYAN " M.M.	
			200431 Cpl. J. DAVIDSON	
			200504 Sjt. M. STEVENSON	
			200553 L/C A. T. ROSS	
			27646 Pt. R. GAVIN	
			200669 Cpl. H. MASTERTON	
			40940 Pt. D. MITCHELL	
			201554 " A. ROBERTSON.	
			Strength.	
			Ret 31/7/18 the strength of the unit was	Without 28 Officers 874 O.R.
				Attached 14 – 118
				Total 42 – 992
			Ret 31/8/18. the strength of the unit was	Without 12 Officers 496 O.R.
				Attached 13 – 182
				Total 25 – 678

App. 1.

5th Battn. H.L.I.

Copy No. 11

ORDER No. 16.

6th August, 1918.

Reference TRENCH MAP B.51.

1. The 5th H.L.I. will relieve the 6th H.L.I. on the 7th August, 1918.

2. "A" Company will relieve "B" Company, 6th H.L.I.
   "B"   "   "   "   "A"   "   "
   "C"   "   "   "   "C"   "   "
   "D"   "   "   "   "D"   "   "

3. "A", "B" and "C" Companies will proceed by OUSE ALLEY. "D" Company will proceed by TOMMY ALLEY.

4. "C" and "D" Companies will move at 9 a.m., "B" Company at 9.30 a.m., "A" Company 10 a.m.

5. Guides will be provided by the 6th H.L.I. as follows:-

   "B" Company at junction of OUSE ALLEY and BROWN Trench
   "A"   "   "   "   "   "   "   "   "
   "C"   "   "   "   "   "   "   POST "
   "D"   "   "   "   "   TOMMY   "   "   "

   ~~Guides will also be provided as above for 6th H.L.I. Advance Party at 7 a.m. 7th August, 1918.~~

6. Each Company will send an Advance Party after the evening meal of 6th August as follows:-

   One Officer and batman per Company.
   One N.C.O. per platoon.
   Two Signallers per Company.
   One runner per Company.

   Headquarters Company will send one N.C.O., two Signallers and two runners.
   Companies will arrange to send to their new Location their cooks and cooking utensils at 7 a.m. on 7th August.

7. Officer i/c Headquarters will arrange that the personnel of Headquarters will move in three parties at 8.30 a.m. 9 a.m. and 9.30 a.m.

8. Officer i/c Signallers will arrange to take over all communication and hand over present communication by 10 a.m.

9. Officer i/c Regimental Scouts will arrange to take over Observation Posts at dawn on 7th August.

10. The Medical Officer will arrange to take over the Aid Post of the 6th H.L.I. by 10.30 a.m. He will also arrange to hand over his present Aid Post and obtain receipt for the Trench Stores.

11. Companies will arrange to take over 170 Lewis Gun Magazines per Company, leaving the same number in their present Area and obtain receipts. The balance of drums, all tin cases, and all buckets will be taken to the new Area. The L.G.O. will arrange to transfer Battalion Reserve of drums to the new Headquarters.

12. Companies will arrange to leave a N.C.O. in the Area to hand over Trench Stores provided the 6th H.L.I. do not send an Advance Party to take these over before the Companies move.

over/

(2)

12(a) Companies will arrange to supply guides for the 6th H.L.I.

"B" Company at junction of OISE ALLEY and BROWN LINE.
"A"   "   "   "   "   "   "   "   "   "
"C"   "   "   "   "   "   "   "   "   "
"D"   "   "   "   " TOMMY   "   "   "   "

Guides will also be provided as above for 6th H.L.I. Advance Parties at 7 a.m. 7th August.

13. Instructions as regards rations will be issued separately.

14. Relief complete will be wired to Battalion Headquarters by the code word "KILTS".

15. Trench Stores, Log Books, Special Maps and Plans will be taken over and receipts given. Duplicates will be sent to Battalion Headquarters by 6 p.m. on 6th August.

16. Statements of Dispositions and Duties with Map will be forwarded to Battalion Headquarters by 6 p.m. on 7th August.

[signature] Lieut.,
Adjutant, 5th Bn. H.L.I.

Copy No 1. O.C. "A" Coy.
        2.   "   "B" "
        3.   "   "C" "
        4.   "   "D" "
        5.   "   6th H.L.I.
        6. 2nd in Command.
        7. O.i/c Sigs., Scouts, L.Gs.
        8. Quartermaster.
        9. Adjutant.
       10. Medical Officer.
       11. War Diary.
       12. War Diary.

War Diary
App II

5th Bn. H.L.I.   Copy No. 7

ORDER No. 17.   7th August, 1918.

Reference Trench Map H.61.

1. A Gas Bomb Discharge will be carried out by the O.Special Company, R.E., from the Railhead at P.16.b.0.8. on the night of 7/8th August or first subsequent night on which the wind is favourable.

2. Zero hour will be 2 a.m.

3. "C" Company will evacuate the area BOW Trench and BOW support by zero minus 45 minutes. "D" Company will evacuate HULL POST by zero minus 30 minutes.

4. "C" Company will withdraw by CURB ALLEY and CURB SIDING and will be accommodated in the disused trench behind the POST LINE running through S.18.c. The garrison of HULL POST will be accommodated in the section of POST trench held by "D" Company.

5. All troops in the POST LINE will wear Box Respirators from zero minus five minutes until the area is declared free of Gas.

6. All Gas curtains on protected Dug-outs will be lowered at zero minus 45 minutes, and unprotected Dug-outs will be evacuated and not re-entered till 12 hours after the Gas Discharge takes place, or until they have been declared safe by the Battalion Gas N.C.O.

7. Evacuated trenches will not be re-occupied until Orders are received from Battalion Headquarters. O.C. "C" Company will, after the withdrawal of his Company, establish his Headquarters in the POST LINE at Headquarters of "D" Company.

8. All Lewis Gun Magazines will be withdrawn with the Guns. All ammunition in area evacuated and in POST LINE will be covered up. Companies will arrange to protect water tanks in their area and to see that petrol tins have their stoppers in.

9. Separate Gas Orders have been issued to the Gas Personnel of the Battalion re the closing out of Dug-outs, Trenches, etc.
O.C. "A" Company will detail two sections to report to Battalion Gas N.C.O. at junction of CURB ALLEY and POST LINE at zero minus 60 minutes.

10. Officer in charge of Signallers will arrange for telephonic communication between Battalion Headquarters and Advanced Battalion Headquarters which will be situated at junction of CURB ALLEY and POST LINE from zero minus 60 minutes until completion of the Operation.
O.C. "C" and "D" Companies will send two runners each to report at Battalion Advanced Headquarters at zero minus 60 minutes.

11. Watches will be synchronised at 10 p.m. Officer in charge Hq. issued. Sig. Sellers will send a watch to Companies for this purpose. The following code will be used:-

Operation will take place to-night..................GOAT.
Operation postponed................................DEER.
Cancel previous operation ordered..................STAY.
Discharge Complete.................................R.E.J.
Line evacuated.....................................FIR.
Manning Line.......................................ELM.
Line re-occupied...................................ACER.

                                         Lieut.,
                                Adjutant, 5th Bn. H.L.I.

(1)

Copy No 1.   O.C. "A" Company.
       2.   "   "B"   "
       3.   "   "C"   "
       4.   "   "D"   "
       5.   O.i/c Signallers.
       6.   Adjutant.
       7.   War Diary.
       8.   "   "

5th H.L.I.

To ALL COMPANIES.

   Reference Battalion Order No 17, para 19, Advanced Battalion Headquarters will be at junction of Road and BUSH ALLEY at B.15.a.95.35., and not as stated in original Order.

                     Lieut.,
7th August, 1916.   Adjutant, 5th Bn. H.L.I.

App. III

6th Battn. D.L.I.   Copy No. 7

Secret   ORDER No.13.   8th August, 1916.

Reference Trench Map WILLERVAL.

1. From 6.30 p.m., 8th August, 1916, the following adjustments will be made in the dispositions in the Battalion Sector:-

2. One platoon of "B" Company, will, for tactical purposes, come under the Control of O.C. "C" Company. O.C. "B" Company will detail the platoon, which should be in command of an Officer, reporting name of Officer and number of platoon to Battalion Headquarters.

3. The platoon of "B" Company will proceed to ROW SUPPORT Trench on receipt of these Orders. O.C. "C" Company will provide a guide to be at the junction of GOSS ALLEY and GOSS RIDING at 6.30 p.m.

4. O.C. "B" Company will arrange to send sufficient Camp Kettles with the platoon, and will arrange that the rations will, until further Orders, be included in the rations of "C" Company. O.C. "C" Company will reorganise his Company in platoon Posts.

        No 1 covering the Block at GOSS ALLEY
        No 2 at mouth of ROW Trench in B.17.c.
        No 3 in ROW Trench where road crosses the trench about
   B.17.c.8.4.
        No 4 in ROW Support where it is joined by GOSS ALLEY.
        No 5 in ROW Trench where it joins GOSS RIDGE.

When these adjustments are made, "C" Company will wire Battalion Headquarters, using the code word "ALLY"

5. O.C. "B" Company will arrange that a Back Sentry Post is established in ROWDY ALLEY about 100 yards forward of BULL POST. O.C. "A" Company will establish a Sentry Post at the broken-down Block in GOSS ALLEY, about 100 yards forward of POST Trench. These Posts will be furnished from Stand-to in the evening till stand-down in the morning, and are established for the purpose of warning the POST LINE of any break through by an enemy raiding party.

                                            Lieut.,
                                   Adjutant, 6th Bn. D.L.I.

Issued at

      Copy No 1.   O.C. "A" Coy.
           2   B
           3   C
           4   D
           5   Adjutant.
           6   Scouts, Sigs., L.Gs.
           7   & 8 War Diary.

Apx IV

5th Bn. H.L.I.　　　　　　　Copy No. 7

Order No. 19.　　　　　　11th August, 1918.

Reference French Map WILLERVAL.

1. From 8.30 p.m., 11th August, 1918, the following adjustments will be made in the Dispositions in the Battalion Sector.

2. The platoon of "B" Company, at present in BOW SUPPORT Trench, will be withdrawn and come under the orders of O.C. "B" Company as part of his Reserve and will be quartered in BAILLEUL.

3. O.C. "C" Coy. will rearrange the advances of the forward zone as follows:-　No 1 Post will remain as at present
　　No 2　"　"　be withdrawn into BOW SUPPORT Trench with the right resting on junction of BOW SUPPORT and OUSE ALLEY.
　　No 3 Post will be moved to the left with the left resting on TOMMY ALLEY
　　No 4 Post will remain as at present.

4. O.C. "B" Coy. will arrange to have one S.O.S. Post in the POST LINE instead of the two Posts as at present.

5. O.C. Coys. concerned will wire Battalion Headquarters when these adjustments are made using the code Word "HERMES".

6. Acknowledge.

Issued at 6.50 p.m.

Copy No 1 O.C. "A" Coy.
　　　　2　　　 "B"
　　　　3　　　 "C"
　　　　4　　　 "D"
　　　　5 Scouts, Sigs, L.Gs.
　　　　6 Adjutant.
　　　　7 & 8 War Diary.

Lieut.
Adjt. 5th Bn. H.L.I.

SECRET.  6th BATTN. ...... Copy No. 10.

WARNING ORDER No. ...

1. The Battalion will move from the present Camp sometime this evening. Time will be notified later.

2. All Officers' Kits and Officers' Mess Stores not required for the evening meal will be stacked near Cookhouse for loading by 6 p.m.

3. The Camp will be cleaned, the men's packs and equipment made up, and O.C. Coys. will report by 6 p.m. that they are ready to move at short notice.

4. Water Carts will be filled immediately and Water Bottles will be filled beginning with "A" Coy. at 6 p.m.

5. <u>Advance Party.</u> The same Advance Party as proceeded yesterday will hold itself in readiness to move at short notice.

6. The Signalling Officer will have all cycles collected outside Orderly Room by 5 p.m.

7. "Q" will arrange to return all Area Stores drawn this morning, reporting when this has been done.

8. The Transport Officer will arrange to inspect all limbers and wagons and report that they are properly loaded.

9. A Loading Party for G.S. wagons will be supplied by the Duty Coy. at 6.15 p.m., reporting to "Q" at that hour.

                                                                    Lieut.,
31st August, 1918.   Adjutant.
Issued at 4.30 p.m.

    Copy No. 1, "A" Coy.   Copy No. 6, Q.M.
     "   " 2, "B" "   "   " 7, T.O.
     "   " 3, "C" "   "   " 8, Adjutant.
     "   " 4, "D" "   "   " 9)
     "   " 5, O.i/c Hqrs.   "   " 10) War Diary.
                                    "   " 11 Sigs.

Copy No.

157th Infantry Brigade Order No 130.
Reference Sheet 51 B. S. W.

Secret.
24th Aug 18.

1. The Army will advance to allow the enemy no respite in their retreat. Accordingly the 52nd Division will conform to the movements of troops on its flanks.

2. The 157th Brigade will pass through the line at present held by the 156th Brigade & which runs approximately from T.c.5.0 to T.a.8.8. The 157th Brigade will attack eastward maintaining touch with the 56th Div which will be attacking on our right. The 157th Brigade will finally assault and consolidate that portion of the Hindenburg line between T.5.a and N.34.d. Both front and support system to be captured. ~~The 56th~~ ~~Div will~~ ~~being~~

3. The 156th Brigade will advance on the left of the 157th Brigade at 7 a.m to the road N32 b 7-6 and to N 26 Cent conforming to movement of 157th Brigade and being echeloned in left rear. ~~The 157th Brigade~~

4. The 6th H.L.I will attack on the right. The 5th H.L.I will attack on the left. The 7th H.L.I and 157th L.T.M.B. (less 2 Sections) C Company 52nd Battalion, M.G.C (less 1 Section) will be in Brigade reserve.

5. The approach march will be timed to bring the two assaulting Battalions into line held by the 156th Brigade by 6.45 a.m. The attack will be carried forward from this line punctually at 7 A.M in conjunction with the 56th Division on our right and our troops on our left, the 156th Brigade following echeloned behind our left FLANK. For the approach march, the 6th & 5th H.L.I will start in Artillery formation from the W side of the Railway running North & South from Poeave. The 6th H.L.I on the right with its right at the junction of the road with the Railway at S3b82 (S6c82) and a frontage of approximately 800 yards. The 5th H.L.I forming up on the left. Advance from here to commence at 4.15 a.m. The advance to be regulated so that the leading lines do not

pass through the 156th Brigade lines until 6.45 A.M.

6. The 7th H.L.I and other troops in Brigade Reserve will move to a position of assembly so as to follow about 1½ miles in rear of 6th H.L.I when the latter Unit moves forward at 4.15 A.M. During the advance the 6th H.L.I will direct.

7. O.C, 157th L.T.M.B. will detail 2 Guns to 6th H.L.I and 2 Guns to the 5th H.L.I. to report on the Railway line at 4 A.M. O.C, 157th L.T.M.B will be prepared to reconnoitre and place the remainder of the guns in position to cover consolidation.

8. O.C, M.G. Coy will detail 1 Section of Guns for an independent mission as a Battery of opportunity. He will with the remainder of his guns take every advantage of covering the advance, 1 Section to be always in Brigade reserve following in rear of 7th H.L.I. After the capture of the final objective he will dispose his guns in depth to cover the consolidation & repel counter-attack.

9. On arrival in the 156th Brigade the 6th H.L.I will at once open

contact with left; 56th Division maintaining it throughout the attack.

10. During the attack the 6th H.L.I will direct. All company officers will work on compass bearings.

11. Rations for 24th plus 1 days Iron Rations will be carried on the man.

12. Frequent information & Situation reports will be sent to Brigade H.Qrs.

13. Prisoners will be sent back under a small escort to behind the Railway at starting point.

14. Brigade H.Qrs will be at S 5 d 83

15. ~~Acknowledge.~~

P.S. Stirling-Cook.
Captain
Brigade Major, 157th Inf Bde

Secret.

154th Inf. Bde. Order No. 135.

24/8/18.

1. 154 Bde will attack at 9.20 a.m. to day under barrage & will capture FONTAINE CROISILLES & continue advance S.E. and take RIENCOURT. U.24.

2. 6th & 7th A.L.I. will be the assaulting Battns. 6th A.L.I. on right 7th A.L.I. on Left & 5th A.L.I. in Reserve

3. Assault Battns will assemble along the line of SUMMIT TR. from T.4.d.6.0 to junction with HINDENBURG SUPPORT Line at N.35.c.3.4. Approach to this line to be concealed from FOOLEY TRENCH.

4. Frontage for 6th A.L.I will be from the RIGHT of this line to where the track crosses it in T.5.& 3.9. Frontage for 7th A.L.I. from there to LEFT, ~~ready to advance from there~~

5. Battns will be ready to advance at 9.20 a.m.

at 9.20 a.m. Barrage will come down on FOOLEY TR. from T.11.a.3.4 to ~~T.5.b.~~ T.5.b.1.9 & remain down to 9.36 a.m by which time the assaulting Battns will have moved forward ~~close~~ close up under the barrage. At 9.36 a.m Barrage & assaulting troops will move forward at 100 yds per 4 mins direct on FONTAINE CROISILLES. 7th A.L.I. ~~directing~~ will direct

6. 155 Bde will mop up HINDENBURG LINE behind our attack as far as FOP LANE in W.I.c. The Left of 7th A.L.I. will be directed on S. end of FONTAINE CROISILLES.

7. 156th Bde will be attacking under a separate Barrage on our

2.

LEFT. The Right of this Bde is being directed on N. end of FONTAINE CROISILLES.

8. The Barrage for 52nd Division will remain on general line of UNA TR. EAST of FONTAINE CROISILLES for 30 minutes after when it will lift & 154 Bde will push on to RIENCOURT & 156 Bde to HENDECOURT.

9. On approaching FONTAINE CROISILLES, 5th A.L.I. in Reserve will (the assaulting Battns) close up 1 Coy, close behind Y A.L.I. to mop up FONTAINE CROISILLES. This Coy will follow the Bde when its mission is finished.

10. While Barrage is on general line UNA TR for 30 minutes, the Assault Battns will re-organise & get their direction for RIENCOURT, the advance to which should be continued without further orders the moment the barrage lifts.

11. 5th A.L.I. in reserve will form up behind the junction of 6th A.L.I. & Y A.L.I. WEST of SUMMIT TRENCH & follow the advance one mile behind.

12. L.S. M Bty will follow as soon as transport can be ~~obtained~~ provided. A.M.G.o will follow close behind the leading wave. The remainder of the guns will support the advance under separate orders fr their C.O.

13. Advance Bde. Hqrs will be established in FAT. SWITCH where track crosses it in T.5.C.3.9. Frequent reports showing location of front lines & progress must be sent in.

14. 56th Divn will be attacking on our RIGHT, forming up in

"SUMMIT TR. post 3 of 6th A.L.).
15. Acknowledge.

[signature]
Captain
Brigade Major, 154th Inf Brigade.

War Diary 5th H.L.I. Copy No. 9.

Secret Order No 20. 15th August 1918

Ref. ROCLINCOURT 10000

1/ The 52nd Division will be relieved in the Line by the 8th and 51st Divisions starting on night of 15th August.

2/ The Batt. will be relieved by the 2nd Southampton Reg. on night 16/17th Aug.

3/ Order of Relief. "A" Coy. 2nd S'ampton Reg. will take over from "A" Coy. 5th H.L.I.
  "B"   from "B"
  "C"   "   "C"
  "D"   "   "D"

4/ Order of march for the incoming unit will be
  "A". B. D. C. H.Q.

5/ Route. 2nd S'ampton Reg.
A Coy. Two left platoons by Tommy Alley
  "   " right   "   "   OUSE "
"B". Two platoons OUSE Alley and DERELICT Trenches.
  2 Support — BAILLEUL Road in B.21.
"C" by OUSE Alley
"D" " TOMMY "

          5th H.L.I.
"A" Coy. by OUSE Alley.
 B " " BAILLEUL Road.
 C " " OUSE Alley.
 D " " TOMMY "

All Companies by OUSE Alley & CONCRETE Road to ROCLINCOURT WEST CAMP where the Battalion will be retained.

2.

Orders to do (contd)

A dressing station for serious casualties will be maintained during crossing at PONT DU JOUR - THELUS ROAD at a separate tent.

Stretcher bearers will start moving from the Divisional Covered Ways & 60 & 63 Alley Bn 6 & 2 at 6 p.m. 16 inst. Orders for same via the Adjts. Bn Batt. Nidor. dress will report to F.S.I.O. Batt. Hars at 5 p.m.

2. Defence holes in Leg Ravine. Inspn from shown. Photographs and all trench stores will be handed over and receipts taken. Details of fencing &c Rations will be specially handed over.

3. In the event of an alarm or enemy appearing the relief troops will back up their keenest defences, reporting their position to Batt. Nidors

9. Impression of whatever be issued to Batt. Hars. by the code word "STUNT".

10. Advance Guard. The following will parade at Batt. Hars at 1.30 p.m. at the moment 16th inst.

	Off.	O/Rs
Major Grand	1	-
Major Forrest	-	7
Signallers	-	2
Boys in	-	2
Sanitary Corporal	-	1
Police	-	4
Company Officers 1 per Coy	4	-
	5	16

Order No 20 (contd).

	Offr	OR
	5	16
Less: 1 pr platoon, 4 pl Coy = 4 pr x 16 = Coy =		20
Batmen 2 pr Coy.		8
Total =	5	44

4. On relief Companies will move independently and will be taken over of Concrete Road b ??? a 3 by Platoon guides supplied by the advance party. These guides will be in position by 9 pm.

12. Dress. Fighting order with gas masks at the alert, also must belt.

13. Baggage. All baggage will be stacked at Bn. H.Q by 6 pm. No baggage will be received after this time. Camp kitchens will be taken to Bn. H.Q by 7 pm.

14. Lewis Gun Ammunition. O.C. "A" "C" & "D" Coys to bring down by Ralway all their camp at 176 drams to TUNNEL Dump by 5.30 pm. Each party of 5avy will consist of 12 m 2 of whom will be Lewis Gunners. This party will report to Police Corporal at TUNNEL dump and will accompany the Cans etc. on the returning ration train from TUNNEL DUMP to ROCLINCOURT. Limbers will meet the train & carry the tin Cans etc. to the new camp. O.C. "B" Coy. will arrange to man-handle his tin Cans & 176 drams to TUNNEL DUMP before five o'sic pm and to hand them over to the Police Corporal. The carrying party less 2 Lewis Gunners will report back to their Coy.

Order No 20 (cont'd)

15. Transport & Ancillaries. These will remain in their present position at ECOIVRES.
16. Nucleus. All Nucleus personnel and details of the Brigade Pioneer Coy will rejoin units on 19th inst.
17. Acknowledge.

	Copy No 1	O.C. "A" Coy
	2	B
	3	C
	4	D
	5	H.Q.
	6	2nd in Command
	7	Adjutant
	8	Adjt. T.Q.A.M.
	9 }	War Diary
	10 }	

Issued at 3.30 a.m. 16/8/18.

Lm A A L Lieut.
Adjt. 5th H.L.I.

15/8/18.

War Diary   2nd H[?]   Copy No 9
            Order No 21   [illegible] 1918

Reference MAROEUIL [?]

1. The Battalion will be relieved [?] around 1HB,
by [?] ... from [illegible] and to CHATEAU DE
LA HAYE Wood.

2. Order of March A O S B C D
Head of column will pass Cross Roads in
A28 a 6.5 at 2 pm.

3. Route much notified later.

4. Dress Fighting order with necessary Kit
carried [?]. Haversack will be worn, and
helmet slung on right shoulder.

5. Dressing Shed will be at B.20 [?]

6. Advance Party consisting of 4 Officers 2 p[er?]
and 30 [?] of All [?] will [proceed?]
[illegible] the [illegible] area
reporting to Area Commander at 12 [?]
The Billet [?] of the Bn will be arranged
by [?] [?]. [?] Billet for
transport line to be seen upon Captain
Watkins at 2 pm.

7. [?] baggage will be stacked on
top of each all on near A Officers Quarters
by 10 am. excepting the Cart [?] required
for midday meal. The Company Mess will be
moved to loading at 6.30 pm. Officers
baggage will be stacked outside Officers

2/

Order No. 31 (contd.)

Tractors at 10 a.m. The loading party will be composed by B Company. One motor lorry will report at 9 a.m. and in addition one lorry. The party for unloading party will be supplied by three or lorry and rations. Lewis Gun Limbers will be taken at 9 a.m. under the Men Buffers in the C of I and will be drawn and forward to the next time at 9 a.m. Ney will be taken daily one each and no fatigue on Sundays.

Copy No 1   O.C. A Coy
     2   B "
     3   C "
     4   D "
     5   H.Q
     6   Adjt
     7   2 i/c O.C.
     8   O.C. Machine
     9
    10   War Diary

                    The Adjt
17-8-18.   Adjt 5 R.H.L.   Lieut

57 B. N.W.
No 2.
C.O.

WAR DIARY
INTELLIGENCE SUMMARY.

5th Bn. H.L.I.

Army Form C. 2118.

Place	Date	Hour	Summary of Events and Information	Remarks and references to Appendices
MERCATEL	19/9	0645	Ref. Map FRANCE Sheet 51 B.S.W. Left BIVOUAC area at MERCATEL and marched to HENIN HILL arriving at SUMMIT TRENCH at 09.45. Remained there overnight training under "Brigade" will remain here till tonight.	
	2/9/18	0500	Left SUMMIT TRENCH and marched to BERG TRENCH remaining there for about one hour. Received orders to continue along BERG TRENCH and proceed via TRIDENT ALLEY to U.26.b.7.4 - BULLECOURT arriving there at 0945. Stood by awaiting further orders. Finally remained overnight.	
BULLECOURT	3/9/18	0510	Left BULLECOURT and proceeded via RIENCOURT to jumping off point in HINDENBURG SUPPORT LINE arriving at 1100. The 167th Inf. Bde. Order No.138 contained the following except which applied to the 5th Bn. H.L.I.:- "The 167th Inf. Bde. will attack today under a barrage at 1107 from "HINDENBURG LINE" in V.26.d. - V.27.c. S and S.E. the QUEANT and PRONVILLE "taking up the line from D.14.a.6 - D.15.a.6 thence along MELBOURNE STREET "to D.10 Central covering QUEANT and PRONVILLE from S. and E. connecting "up with Guards Division at D.11 Central". The 7th. & 8th H.L.I. will form the "advancing battalions attaching in following - 5th H.L.I. on RIGHT from S. thro' E. end "of QUEANT & HINDENBURG SUPPORT LINE in D.14 a.6 - D.15 a. 7th H.L.I. "on left attacking thro' PRONVILLE." QUEANT and PRONVILLE were found to be evacuated. Barrage was cancelled and Bn. pushed off at 11.45 attacking through EAST of QUEANT against HINDENBURG FRONT LINE which we carried on reaching about 12.20 without opposition. Bn. reorganised and orders received for Bn. to advance to + map ref: the 1st and 2nd lines of the HINDENBURG FRONT LINE EAST W.26.D to TROPOLE COPSE eventually occupying these	

1577 Wt.W10791/1773 500,000 1/15 D.D.&L. A.D.S.S./Forms/C.2118.

Army Form C. 2118.

WAR DIARY
or
INTELLIGENCE SUMMARY. 5th Bn. H.L.I.

46/2

(Erase heading not required.)

Instructions regarding War Diaries and Intelligence Summaries are contained in F. S. Regs., Part II. and the Staff Manual respectively. Title pages will be prepared in manuscript.

Place	Date	Hour	Summary of Events and Information	Remarks and references to Appendices
NEAR INCHY	3/9/16		Three lines in (Ref Map 1/20000 57CNE) D17 and D18. 2/Lt. L.B. HILLSON rejoins transport lines from UK leave. 2/Lt. T.B. WEIGHT leave " " " proceeding on UK leave	
	4/9/18 5/9/18 6/9/18		Holding line at D17 and D18. Intermittent shelling with HE and Gas Shells (Green X)	
	7/9/16		Lieut. M.D. NICOLSON rejoins Bn from BoD & takes over duty as Signalling Officer. Lieut W. Cumming proceeds to join 3rd Army Musketry School, FORT MAHON. Received orders to withdraw & rejoin Brigade area near ST. LEGER. Left our position in line at 0700 during heavy concentration of yellow × Gas Shells and arrived ST. LEGER about 11 A.M. 2/Lt. W. Linton joins Bn at ST. LEGER. Casualties during three 14 6 340 Reft. 5 O/R wounded by shell fire 45 O/R Gassed - mustard. Reinforcements: Major to Jenkins, 2/Lt. A. Barker, 2/Lieut R. Park.	
	8/9/18		Proceed on UK leave :- 2/Lieut R. Park. Back at ECOUST Reinforcements:- Capt W.F.H. Donald M.C. 9th H.L.I. 2/Lieut Shore.	
	9/9/18 10/9/18 11/9/16 12/9/18 13/9/16		Training under Coy arrangements, re-equipping etc. 2/Lt. R. Lumsden rejoins from UK leave.	

A 3834 Wt. W4973/M687 750,000 8/16 D D & L Ltd. Forms/C.2118/13.

WAR DIARY
INTELLIGENCE SUMMARY

Army Form C. 2118.

5th Bde HZI. 407/3

(Erase heading not required.)

Place	Date	Hour	Summary of Events and Information	Remarks and references to Appendices
ST. LEGER	18/9/18		General training.	
			Afternoon. Congratulatory visit by 17th Corps Commander, Sir Chas Ferguson Bart. The following officers were accompanied from 26th Divn. Army Musketry Camp. HOTRINGHAM. Capt. R. H. Harrison Lieut. J. Brewer The nominated officer proceeds on U.K. leave. Capt. J. C. Morris	
	18/9/18	1000	Divine Service.	
		1500	Governor Commander, Gen. Sir Chas. visits Bde. Hqrs. the friend Military Medals to members of Bde. NCOs and men as under of the 5th HZI. were inspected. H.H.S. are the Corps-Brine Commander service that their congratulations to conveyed to the recipients. N° 200377 Sergt. John Logan "C" Cy. N° 200431 Corpl. John Donaldson "C" N° 276648 Pte. Robert Gavin "B" N° 201652 " Andrew Robertson "B" N° 202105 " Chas. Rupt. Sturgeon "D" N° 200501 Cpl. Michael Hanneran "C" N° 40940 Pte. David Benjamin N° 200553 Lc Ale. Long Ross H2 N° 200307 Pte. George Clark H2	
			Lieut. H. D. Nicolson proceeded to 9th Corps Signalling XVIII Corps School HARESQUEL	

WAR DIARY
INTELLIGENCE SUMMARY

4044   5th Bn H.L.I.

(Erase heading not required.)

Army Form C. 2118.

Place	Date	Hour	Summary of Events and Information	Remarks and references to Appendices
	16/9/18		Took over line in HINDENBURG SUPPORT LINE between INCHY and MOEUVRES at midnight from 1st Bn MUNSTER FUSILIERS. 'B' and 'C' Coys in front line and outposts in shell hole. 'B' and 'D' Coy in support.	
	17/9/18		Heavy shelling on HINDENBURG SUPPORT LINE all day.	
		18.30	Heavy enemy bombardment put down on MOEUVRES extending to front of 'C' Coy coming down behind support line. Troops on our RIGHT were driven in necessitating a defensive flank being formed by 'D' Coy from LEFT post of 'C' Coy which had been driven back but had reoccupied its position at (Ref map 57c NE) E.14.2.10.85 down HOBART STREET to E.13 Central. Reserves to the E.13 had been found that land with right post of 'C' Coy had been lost. Frequent patrols and parties attempting to reach this post were driven off by enemy. Columns howling about by enemy on right were all driven off. A block being placed in front of HOBART STREET TRENCH post in which last post 'C' Coy was relieved by 'D' Coy. Withdrawing to dugout at E.13 b 20.05. Heavy shelling all night.	
		About 7pm	Lt + adjt T.B. Clark was wounded and Capt. K. Ross R.A.M.C. mortally wounded in WARBURG STREET.	
			The following officers report at Transport lines:- Lieut Muir Milne from GHQ Lewis Gun Course. 2/Lt J.S. McKenzie from UK leave.	

19. TOUQUET

WAR DIARY
or
INTELLIGENCE SUMMARY.

(Erase heading not required.)

Army Form C. 2118.

5th Bn H.L.I.

Place	Date	Hour	Summary of Events and Information	Remarks and references to Appendices
NEAR MOEUVRES	18/9/18		Capt T. S. WILSON joins Bn. vice Capt to have wounded.	
			HINDENBURG LINE heavily shelled all day. Attempts to find missing post of "C" Coy. were all driven off by enemy. "D" Coy on RIGHT relieved by "B" Coy.	
	19/9/18		Heavy enemy shelling all day. An attack was ordered to retake MOEUVRES; the was carried out by 155th Inf Bde on our RIGHT with two Companies 7th H.L.I. to attack EIL Central. One Coy of 7th H.L.I. being ordered to re-establish the post occupied by RIGHT post "C" Coy. Bombardment to commence 1900 for 5 minute barrage to move forward afterwards 100 yards each 4 minutes. "A" Coy was ordered to carry the cut pinpring off from HOBART STREET. They were held up first short of objective by machine gun fire from LEFT, which being the flank on our left at flank of barrage. The bombardment had not been sufficiently effective. "D" Coy was ordered to support "A" Coy, and having done so the missing post of "C" Coy under Corporal DAVID HUNTER was enabled to be relieved. The post could not be maintained owing to strong hostile attacks. The Bn was in process of being relieved by the 25th Bn. Canadians which was completed about 12 midnight, the Bn. proceeding to Bivouac Area near MORUIL.	

WAR DIARY or INTELLIGENCE SUMMARY

Army Form C. 2118.

5th Bn. H.L.I.

46/6

Place	Date	Hour	Summary of Events and Information	Remarks and references to Appendices
	19/9/18		The following casualties were sustained by the Bn. for those from 16th to 19th Sept.	
			Killed :- Capt. W.F. McDonald 9th att 5th H.L.I. on 19th inst.	
			9 O/Ranks.	
			Wounded :- 2/Lieut A. Bryson 5 H.L.I. on 19th inst.	
			Lieut & Adjutant T.B. Clarke 18th "	
			Capt. K. McK. Ross R.A.M.C. 18th "	
			24 O/Ranks	
			Gassed :- 7 O/Ranks	
			Missing :- 4 O/Ranks	
			Sick (to Hospital) 2/Lieut Dunan (shell-shock)	
NOEUIL	20/9/18	0300	Bn arrived at Bivouac Area near NOEUIL.	
	21/9/18		Cleaning up training. Nucleus under Major D.E. Brand DSO rejoined Bn.	
			The following officers joined the Bn from U.K.:-	
			2/Lt E. Guest, 2/Lt E. Schroeder; 2/Lt R. Erskine; 2/Lt D.G. Munro; 2/Lt J. Morrison	
			Lieut S.H. Fraser proceeded to 3rd Army Rest Camp.	
	22/9/18		Training. Bathe at ECOUST. 2/Lieut J.B. Wright rejoined Bn from U.K. leave.	

Army Form C. 2118.

WAR DIARY
or
INTELLIGENCE SUMMARY.
(Erase heading not required.)

5th Bn. H.L.I.

1481/7

Instructions regarding War Diaries and Intelligence Summaries are contained in F.S. Regs., Part II. and the Staff Manual respectively. Title pages will be prepared in manuscript.

Place	Date	Hour	Summary of Events and Information	Remarks and references to Appendices
	23/9/18		Forenoon training. Received draft of 75 O.R.	
	24/9/18		Received orders that Bn. would take over the line on RIGHT of MOEUVRES on night of 24/25th Sept. Lt-Col Rochera & Mackie 2/Lt Guest proceeded to new area in forenoon reconnoitred the line. Bn. joined by Battalion Major Roach, 2/Lt Wilson & A Coy Comdr - Lieut. Milne A Cpl. King B. Capt. Straughan C 2/Lt Dundass D Coy reconnoitred line before taking over Coy in. Battalion moved off about 6 P.M. Capt. Straughan + 2/Lt Allison relieved Baton from Cannes. The Bn. relieved 60 H.L.I. and occupied position without loss.	
	25/9/18		During the line - nothing to report.	
	26/9/18	000	2/Lt Park rejoins Battalion from M.C. Leave. Conference of C.O.'s by Brig. Gen. Hamilton Moore C.M.G. D.S.O. held at 5th Bn. H.Q'rs to discuss general attack contemplated on 27th inst. Received orders for the attack our relative position with other formations being as follows:- from LEFT to RIGHT Canadian Division, 63rd Inf. Divn, 52nd Division (inc 155 Bde and 5th H.L.I. Civis/c Divisions). Task allotted to 5th H.L.I. was to capture	

WAR DIARY
or
INTELLIGENCE SUMMARY.

Army Form C. 2118.

A O/8   58 Br. H.Z.I

Place	Date	Hour	Summary of Events and Information	Remarks and references to Appendices
	27/9/18		(05:20) Two foots arrived at F.16.a.8.7 and F.20.c.80.15 between zero and zero + 5. These foots were accurate without opposition. The attack being pushed forward successfully resulted in no material change in the Brushwood location.	
	28/9/18		Orders were received to move back to trench system running NORTH from MOEUVRES ROAD to CAMBRAI– BAPAUME Road (Ref map. 57cNE) F.25.b & d.	
	29/9/18		Same location. Being resting.	
	30/9/18		Casualties for period 24th to 30th Sept 1918. Killed 5 O/Ranks Wounded 17 O/Ranks	

Army Form C. 2118.

WAR DIARY
— or —
INTELLIGENCE SUMMARY. 5th Br HLI

4/9

(Erase heading not required.)

Place	Date	Hour	Summary of Events and Information	Remarks and references to Appendices
			At 21/8/18 the strength of the unit was:-	
			with rear 12 officers 496 O/ranks	
			attached 13 " 182 "	
			25 Officers 678 O/ranks	
			At 30/9/18 the strength of the unit was:-	
			with unit 26 officers 530 O/ranks	
			attached 10 " 140 "	
			36 Officers 670 O/ranks	
			The following recommendations for awards were submitted to Brigade	
			Officers :- Capt Ronald N. Morrison recommended for bar to M.C. or D.S.O.	
			Lieut Stuart M. Grier " " M.C.	
			O/ranks No 43247 Cpl David Ferguson Hunter " " V.C.	
			" 200062 Pte John F. Philip " " D.C.M.	
			" 202014 A/Cpl J Rae " " D.C.M.	
			" 200474 L/Cpl George Meiklejohn " " D.C.M.	

WAR DIARY
or
INTELLIGENCE SUMMARY. 5th Bn. H.L.I.

(Erase heading not required.)

Army Form C. 2118.

Place	Date	Hour	Summary of Events and Information	Remarks and references to Appendices
40/11			Captain L. H. WATSON. awarded Military Cross	
			No 200377 Sgt. John Logan "C" Coy awarded M.M.	
			" 200431 Cpl. John Lawson C " M.M.	
			" 27616 Pte. Peter Cairns B " M.M.	
			" 201574 " Andrew Robertson B " M.M.	
			" 202105 " Geo P Hogan D " M.M.	
			" 200501 Corpl. Michael Stevenson C " M.M.	
			" 40910 Pte. David R. Mitchell D " M.M.	
			" 200307 " George Clark H.Q. Sig. (C Coy) " M.M.	
			" 200553 Sgt. Alexander T Ross H.Q. "C" Coy " M.M.	
			" 241324 Sgt. L Campbell "C" Coy " D.C.M.	
			" 55853 Pte. G Booth "B" Coy " M.M.	
			" 200959 Corpl. H. Waterlow "D" Coy Longfoot " M.M.	

Army Form C. 2118.

WAR DIARY
or
INTELLIGENCE SUMMARY.   5th Bn H.L.I.
(Erase heading not required.)

40/10

Place	Date	Hour	Summary of Events and Information	Remarks and references to Appendices
			Recommendations (continued)	
			No. 203406 Cpl. Jno. McFarlane recommended for DCM	
			" 200072 " James Chalin MM	
			" 200182 L/Cpl. William McElwee MM	
			" 55202 Pte. Brian Nee MM	
			" 41617 " Ralph Cox MM	
			" 40266 " James Fleming MM	
			" 200589 " Henry Chandler MM	
			" 55969 " Wesley Macallan MM	
			" 55970 " William James MM	
			" 201725 " Charles Clarency MM	
			" 50153 " James Aspuna MM	
			" 200086 " Simon Ross MM	
			" 23166 " Samuel Irvine MM	
			The following awards were made to the Battalion and the Corps & Divnl Commanders stated their congratulations conveyed to the recipients.	

5/c N·E
1/20000

57c N·E
1/20000

15th M.L.9.
Oct. 1918

On His Majesty's Service.

WAR DIARY.

1/5th Battalion HIGHLAND LIGHT INFANTRY.

OCTOBER 1918.

41/1. 1/5th H.L.I.

WAR DIARY or INTELLIGENCE SUMMARY

Army Form C. 2118.

(Erase heading not required.)

Place	Date	Hour	Summary of Events and Information	Remarks and references to Appendices
S.W. of CAMBRAI	1-10-18		Major THORBURN and Company Commanders reconnoitred line to be taken over from 63rd Bn SW of CAMBRAI to night. Batt moved with Brigade at 12.20. Took over trenches in support to 155 Bgde. Relief complete by 17.00. Mules move to transport lines at CANTAING. Roads near CANAL L'ESCAUT shelled during relief, but no casualties incurred. Conference of Coy. Commanders with reference to projected attack on NIERGNIES and AWOINGT with 6th & 7th H.L.I. to take place on the morning of the 2nd October.	57 C.N.E. maps. 10000. and 57 B.N.W.
"	2-10-18		Quiet until about 1530 am shelled, chief hit on our front wounding Capt. H.L. STRACHAN, Lt. W.H. MILNE, 2nd Lt. T.A. ALLISON, 2nd Lt. J. WHIMSTER, and killing C.S.M. JONES and wounding 13 O.R. The shell struck C. Coy. Hqrs. 2nd Lt. H. FRASER & Lt. CARMICHAEL 2nd M.C., Capt. KING M.C. and 2nd Lt. WILSON joined from Transport lines.	
"	3-10-18		Day quiet. CAPT. KING went to Melbourne. Capt. MAIN reported. One O.R. on leave fell out of control in our lines, the filot was wounded. Warning order for relief of 155 Bgde by 157th.	

WAR DIARY or INTELLIGENCE SUMMARY

Army Form C. 2118.

41/2   1/5th H.L.I.

Place	Date	Hour	Summary of Events and Information	Remarks and references to Appendices
			Bgde. received (Appendix No. 1)	Appendix No. 1.
S.W. of CAMBRAI A.1	4.10.17		C.O. attended conference at Bgde. Hqrs. regarding the relief, subsequently he was evacuated sick. Major BRAND arrived from Transport lines and assumed command. Relief commenced after dusk, it was complicated as the 155 Bgde. had had an unsuccessful attack on FAUBERG DE PARIS and their companies were mixed. We took over from 5th B.S.F. & 8th R.S. and elements of the 4th K.O.S.B. We were informed that the line taken over consisted of posts and a redoubt in A.27.a and that these could not be visited by day owing to enemy M.G. fire. A. Coy. took over the Redoubt with C. Coy. in support. A Coy took over posts on the left & D. Coy. with B. Coy. in support at PARIS COPSE. 9hrs.	
S.W. of CAMBRAI	5.10.16		Relief completed received at 02.00. Bat. Hqrs. established in Pill Box with day out on road at A.20.c.10.25. Intermittent shelling all day. At 14.00 received normal at A.2b.h.2b take in 200 yards more of trench S.E. Off. h 2. order (147.A.23)	Off. h 2.
			By redoubt held by D. Coy. and twenty horse in A.27.a.9.6.	

Army Form C. 2118.

WAR DIARY
or
INTELLIGENCE SUMMARY.
(Erase heading not required.)

1/5th H.L.I.

41/3

Place	Date	Hour	Summary of Events and Information	Remarks and references to Appendices
S.W.B. CAMBRAI			Lost orders for this detailing D. Coy. (Capt. h°3) in the morning visited B Coy. but found it impossible to go to the other Coys. as no C.T.'s had been formed and there was no winter opening even from trench at 1800 received verbal orders subsequently confirmed cancelling the projected operation by D. Coy. but C.O. 7 H.L.I. and made arrangements for them relieving us on night of 6/7th October. O.C. D. Coy. (Capt. MORRISON) sent in reports from his patrols during the night from which it was definitely established that the redoubt in A.27.d. had not been handed over but only a small post. So it on the death reported this to Bgde. Warning order received that we would be relieved to-night by 1st Royal Inniskilling Fusiliers (57th Bgde.) Their advance party arrived at 2000 and arrangements to relief were made. BHQ	Appx. N° 3.
E.26.	6.10.18		Relief complete at 0230. Coys. moved independently after relief to	
W. of CANAL DU NORD			Area previously occupied by us West of CANAL DU NORD in E.26.1. Last Coy arrived at 0700. Day spent resting. BHQ	

WAR DIARY or INTELLIGENCE SUMMARY

Army Form C. 2118.

4/1/4

Place	Date	Hour	Summary of Events and Information	Remarks and references to Appendices
	7.10.18		Received orders to send billeting party forward. Batt. moved less transport, which entrained in the morning, at 12.30, to VAUX VRACOURT and entrained for PETIT HOUVAIN at 2000.	
LIGNEREUIL	8.10.18		Battalion arrived at PETIT HOUVAIN at 0700 marching LIGNEREUIL at 1230. The remainder of the day was spent in getting billets cleaned and resting.	
	9.10.18		2/Lieut DE LAVISON reported to the battalion as reinforcement. The whole of the day spent in cleaning of clothing, equipment & all the men receiving hot baths and change of clothing. Major A. CRAWFORD at joined the battalion from U.K. and assumed command of the Battalion. Major DE BRAND taking over 2nd in command. Capt H. DAWSON (A.M.C.) joined the Battalion & took over from Capt. T.S. WILSON who has left to U.K. leave. 2/Lieut R.E.S. & Lieut PRICE joined unit as reinforcement. 2/Lieut DIVENS D.G. to Hospital.	
	10.10.18		Commenced platoon training. Capt R.H. MORRISON M.C. proceeded on U.K. leave.	O.L.
	11.10.18		Training. Capt H.L. STRANGHAN rejoined from hospital.	O.L.
	12.10.18		Platoon training. Special attention being directed to Platoon Schemes.	O.L.

Army Form C. 2118.

WAR DIARY
or
INTELLIGENCE SUMMARY.

5th Br. H.L.I.   41/5

(Erase heading not required.)

Place	Date	Hour	Summary of Events and Information	Remarks and references to Appendices
LIGNEREUIL	13.10.18		Divine Service in Church. Evening. Revd. McInnes officiating. 2/Lt T.L. WEST joined the Bn. as a reinforcement from UK.	OL
	14.10.18		Continued Platoon training - 2 Coys firing on range. 2/Lt T.A. ALLISON reports from Hospital Capt H.L. STRAUGHAN proceeds on UK leave and 2/Lt L.S. HULSON to rest camp AUDRESSELLES	OL
	15.10.18		Company + Platoon training. Aeroplane height demonstration plane report at	OL
			At height of 1000. 2000. 3000 feet showing WR.G. Green Red Very lights at respective heights in order to assist troops to estimate ranges.	
	16.10.18		Company training. 2/Lt E. PARK proceeded to HE Lewis Gun Course LE TOUQUET	OL
	17.10.18		Company + Platoon training	2/Lt
	18.10.18		Training orders received that Brigade moved move to ST. ELOI. Day spent in preparing for move	
	19.10.18		Left LIGNEREUIL at 1930 proceeded by route march to ST. ELOI leaving at 2nd day for a meal en route. Arrived at ST. ELOI at 1600 and found accommodation in DURHAM RUSSE, LANCASTER Camps.	
			Lieut I. CARMICHAEL DSO MC left unit at LIGNEREUIL proceeding on UK leave	OL
	20.10.18		Brigade orders No 612 received ordering move from ST ELOI to HENIN-LIETARD	
			Left ST ELOI at 0900 proceeded by route march to HENIN-LIETARD arriving at 1230 for midday meal. Resuming march at 1530 2/Lt T.A. ALLISON proceeded on UK leave	OL

WAR DIARY
INTELLIGENCE SUMMARY.

41/6   5th Br. H.L.I.

Army Form C. 2118.

(Erase heading not required.)

Place	Date	Hour	Summary of Events and Information	Remarks and references to Appendices
HENIN-LIETARD	21/10/18		Brigade Order no 153 received ordering continuation of march EASTWARDS.	A
PLANQUE			Left HENIN-LIETARD at 0900 proceeding to PLANQUES arriving in billets at 1100	
			Lieut W. CUMMING, Asst. I.O. proceeded to Brigade Headquarters to understudy	A
			Brigade Major	A
	22.10.18		Day spent in cleaning billets, equipment, etc.	A
	23.10.18		Platoon training. Capt A.C. King proceeded on UK leave	A
	24.10.18		Left PLANQUES at 0900 proceeded to FLINES via FLERS - DOUAI - FAUBG - MONCHY	A
			RACHES - PETIT BRAILLON - MONTREVIL arriving FLINES at 1400	
			An Saulotobily billeted in town. Lieut J.R WRIGHT proceeded to Hospital	
			3 other R.O.R&N proceeded to hine Gun Course, LE TOUQUET.	
FLINES	25/10/18		Day spent in cleaning billets refitting training	A
	26.10.18		Warning Orders. 52nd Division will relieve 12th Division in line on night 28/29 inst	A
			The 157th Inf. Bde. group less 413th R.E. two plns one coy MG Bn. will march	
			to billets in LANDAS tomorrow 27th inst.	
			Major D.E. Cood proceeded on UK leave	A

Army Form C. 2118.

WAR DIARY
INTELLIGENCE SUMMARY.

(Erase heading not required.)

5th Bn. H.L.I.

41/7

Place	Date	Hour	Summary of Events and Information	Remarks and references to Appendices
LANDAS	28/10/18	12.15	Left FLINES at 12.15 & marched by route march to BURBOTIN near LANDAS via COUTICHES - ORCHIES - RUE D'ORCHIES - LANDAS. Night spent in billets	OL
LUCELLES	29.10.18		Left LANDAS & marched by route march to LECELLES via Coys made at VIEUX CONDE - RUMEGIES. Bn. billeted en route by Bde. Commander. Capt R.H. Morrison M.C. rejoined from U.K. leave.	OL
	29.10.18		Cleaning kits & equipment etc.	OL
	30.10.18		Bn. Coy training resumed.	OL
	31.10.18		Bn. Coy training.	OL

Comparative Strength Table

Strength as at 30/9/18 .... 26 officers 530 O.R.
add Increase (a) details overleaf 17 " 179 "
                                   43 " 709 "
Less Decrease (b) details overleaf 19 " 298 "
                                   24 officers 411 O.R.

WAR DIARY / INTELLIGENCE SUMMARY

Army Form C. 2118.

5th Bn HLI

41/8

Place	Date	Hour	Summary of Events and Information						Remarks and references to Appendices
	31/10/18		(a) Increase		Officers	O/R	(b) Decrease	Officers	O/R
			1	From Hospital	3	62	1 To Hospital sick 4		80
			2	" Leave	3	78	2 " " wounded 4		11
			3	" Course	3	31	3 " Goo		1
			4	Rest Camp	1		4 " Reid		1
			5	Rct from 2/5 Rg Engr	3		5 " Missing		2
			6	Reinforcements	7	5	6 " Courses of Instr 1		26
					17	179	7 " Leave		166
							8 " Rest Camp	1-	3
							9 To UK for Commis.		1
							10 " " Base under age		1
							11 " " for Med. Board		1
							12 " To LTMB		1
							13 " Struck off		1
							14 " Brigade H9		3
								19	298

Army Form C. 2118.

WAR DIARY
or
INTELLIGENCE SUMMARY. 5th Bn. H.L.I.

4/1/9

(Erase heading not required.)

Place	Date	Hour	Summary of Events and Information	Remarks and references to Appendices
	31/10/18		The following awards for valour were published during the month	
			Victoria Cross.	
			N° 43247 Corpl (a/Sgt) D.F. HUNTER	
			Distinguished Conduct Medal.	
			N° 200652 Pte J. PHILLIPS	
			" 203406 " D. MCFARLANE	
			" 53770 " W. JONES	
			" 41617 " W. GRAY	
			" 40666 " J. FLEMING	
			" 200474 Sergt J. HEIKLEJOHN	
			Military Medal.	
			N° 201014 Pte (a/L/Cpl) I. ROSS	
			" 200066 " L. ROSS	
			" 21306 " S. IRVINE	
			" 50155 " J. ALFORD	
			" 204846 Corpl (A/Sgt) J. CREEK	

Army Form C. 2118.

WAR DIARY
or
INTELLIGENCE SUMMARY. 5th Bn H.L.I

(Erase heading not required.)

41/10

Place	Date	Hour	Summary of Events and Information	Remarks and references to Appendices
	31/10/18		The undernoted officer was awarded Bar to Military Cross.	
			Capt R H MORRISON. M C	
			Cranford Majr	
			Comdg 5th H'Hland Lyht Infantry	
	31.10.18			

… / …

WAR DIARY
or
INTELLIGENCE SUMMARY.
(Erase heading not required.)

Army Form C. 2118.

5th Bn HLI

42/1

Place	Date	Hour	Summary of Events and Information	Remarks and references to Appendices
LECELLES	1/11/18		Platoon & Company training	
			Lieut J.A. McCrum & Capt I Walker joined as reinforcements.	
			Lieut J.G. Alexander left unit to join 9th (S.R.) Bn	
			Lieut S. Ashton to Hospital	
"	2.11.18		Platoon Company training.	vr
"	3.11.18		Platoon Company training. Anti-tank Demonstration	vr
			Warning order for Duty 35 march	
			Capt Hughes returned from UK leave.	vr
			Major Lawson D.S.O. took command, proceeded at 0930 to reconnoitre S.O.S.	
ST AMAND	4.11.18		Billeting Area. Unit moved from BOURBOTIN at 1300, proceeded to ST AMAND	
			took over from 2nd Devons, 8th Divn in the village arriving 1430	
			Lieut Wilson rejoined from Rest Camp	vr
			Bathing & cleaning of kits.	
"	5.11.18		Coast Walker took over from Major St Amand. A Coy Nothing nor Coy reports ok.	
			Major Gaylord proceeded to Div Hqrs for conference. Divn' HQtrs proceeded to L.G. Country	vr
			FRESSIN	

14 B.
2 sheets

vr

WAR DIARY or INTELLIGENCE SUMMARY

Army Form C. 2118.

42/2 .... 3rd Bn. H.L.I.

Place	Date	Hour	Summary of Events and Information	Remarks and references to Appendices
ST AMAND	6.11.18		Capt. Gaylor & Capt. Strachan proceeded to reconnoitre line to be taken over by C/Coy	
			Lieut. Stone proceeded to reconnoitre position to be occupied by "B" Coy	
			"A" Coy 159 reserve	WR
"	7.11.18		Morning Order O.H. 76. No 1st part confirmed	
			"B" Coy forced intake over dispositions of 7th H.L.I. - Right Coy	
"			" " " " " " - Left Coy + Rt. of 8th Canadians	
			Lieut. E. GUEST to 1st Army Laundry School BOULOGNE	
			Bn. Hq. STAGGARD at 1400 proceeded via CUBERY ODOMEZ to Q23 b 9.9.	WR
ODOMEZ	8.11.18		"C" Coy sent out 1 platoon under Lieut. Wilson to enter CONDE who reported all clear	
			Code word "HUTT" received & Unit proceeded to ODOMEZ	WR
			Capt. Miller C.F. proceeded on UK leave	
HARCHIES	9.11.18		Left ODOMEZ at 0600 proceeded to CHENE RAOUL arriving 1100. Shame at 1330 to HARCHIES	WR
			White mnjr. Allura tonight	
			Lieut. Carmichael reports from UK leave. Lieut. S.M. DOWNIE from Unit as reinforcement	
			Entered BELGIUM at 1435	WR

Army Form C. 2118.

WAR DIARY
or
INTELLIGENCE SUMMARY.

5. R. Bn. H.L.I.

M 2/3

(Erase heading not required.)

Instructions regarding War Diaries and Intelligence Summaries are contained in F. S. Regs., Part II. and the Staff Manual respectively. Title pages will be prepared in manuscript.

Place	Date	Hour	Summary of Events and Information	Remarks and references to Appendices
GARENNES	10.11.18		Bn. left HARCHIES at 0630 Marched via VILLE POMMEREUIL HOUTRAGE VILLEROT VACRESSE G	
	11.11.18		GARENNES – J.1. d.77 – when stilled H.M.G. fire Renewed this morning.	
			Lieut. R.G. MORTON leave on from U.K. no new increment	W
W. of MONS	11.11.18		Bn. left GARENNES at 0730 proceeding Wake up line on MONS – JURBISE Road	
			Received word of Armistice at 0950 – Armistice to commence 1100	
			Battalion Halts in front of MONS ROAD.	W
	12.11.18		Position of Unit – D.29 a 7.4.	
			Lieut. Brown proceed on Sick leave W. Ja allen returned from U.K. leave	W
ERBISOEUL	13.11.18		Relieved by 6th H.L.I. shortly ave Her billets in ERBISOEUIL arriving 17.00	
			Capt Daily returned Unit from leave TOHN MAJOR ST AMAND.	W
			Capt King returned Unit from U.K. leave	W
	14.11.18		Ma[j] Glen[?] cleaning equipment. Warning Order by Army Commander	
			officially ending MOBS about 0100 on 15th – following births will attd. 3.52 H.L.I. 80.6.	W
	15.11.18		Party of 150 attracts 5th H.L.I. 100 from 6th and 50 from 7th sents Major Pahlo	
			Area siet[?] Marched first in MONS with Band returned from U.K. leave	
			Lt. Bt. Livers returned from Hospital. 2/Lt. J.R. N. Young joined as reinforcement from U.K. and to Battoe to D. Coy.	W

(1988) D. D. & L., London, E.C. Wt. W869/M1672 350,000 4/17 Sch. 52a. Forms/C.2118/14

WAR DIARY or INTELLIGENCE SUMMARY

Army Form C. 2118.

4/3/Y.   5.7. Bn H.L.I.

Place	Date	Hour	Summary of Events and Information	Remarks and references to Appendices
ERQUELINNES	16.11.18		Station Company Parade + Cleaning of Equipment etc.	wt
	17.11.18		Special Sons Thanksgiving Service at which 100 other 5.7 H.L.I. under Call Roll marrow were present.	wt
	18.11.18		Inspection of Arms, Stables, Harness, Scaling, Bunkers, Cookers etc by Brigadier G.B. Price C.B. Comdg. 15th Bde commanding 53rd Inf Bde.	
			Lieut. J. McIntyre proceeded on Local Leave.	
			Went A.D. Cockburn strained on re-inforcement from U.K. posted to C. Coy. Battalion Drill under Major Crawford at 11:30.	wt
	19.11.18		Company Parades 9.10.30 Battalion Drill 11-12	wt
			Major R.G. Kent evacuated to Hospital	
	20.11.18		Company Parades 9-11 Battalion Drill 11-12	
			Lieut. Mather rejoined Unit from Hospital. Lieut Dumfries proceeded to leave for Scotland.	wt
	21.11.18		Battalion Drill 9-10. Company Parades 10-11. Ceremonial Drill 11-12.30	
			Lecture by Lieut. Morrison, Divisional Educational Officer, on "Waterloo" held in village church.	wt
	22.11.18		Ceremonial Drill 9-10. Company Drill 10-11. Educational Scheme commenced.	wt
			11.30 Lecture Call for men attended by 30 pupils	

WAR DIARY
or
INTELLIGENCE SUMMARY.

Army Form C. 2118.

5th Bn. H.L.I.

47/5

Place	Date	Hour	Summary of Events and Information	Remarks and references to Appendices
ERBISOEUIL	18-11-18		Inspection of Huts made that by B.G.C. Lt. Col. G. Muir, C.O. B. Adjt. G.B. Price, O.C. B. C.M.B. O.S.O.	WA
"	20-11-18		at 1000 on Drill Ground Divine Service 1030	WA
			Undernoted officers proceeded to L.G. School assembling at CHATEAU DE BRUISSERT —	
		2 a.m. 1500	Lieut. MATHER, 2/Lt. M.S. DOWNIE, LIEUT SHEDDEN	
		2/Lt SPROAT, 2/Lt COCKBURN, Lieut R.S MORTON, 2/Lt T.R.M. SLING		WA
"	25-11-18		Battalion Company training	
			Lecture by B.G.C. to all officers C.S.M's Serjts & others to representing "The Platoon" at	
		1730 in Recreation Room		
			Lieut Bowie Homes for local leave	WA
"	26-11-18		Battalion & Company training	WA
"	27-11-18		Company training Lecture & Demonstration by R.E. officer on "String String Bond" and Erecting Huts	
			Lieut J.G McKenzie returned from local leave	WA
"	28-11-18		Lt Col Crawford proceeded on local leave	WA
"	29-11-18		Bathing Rev L.R Lawson Lewis Bath 9th Welsh provided 20 Wired to 9th Bn. Lieut Mitchell proceeded on local leave & Lewis Killen took over duties of Adjt.	WA

R.D.A. (To London) D.D.&L. London E.C. Sch. 52a. Forms/C/2118/14
(A589) Wt. W807/M1672. 350,000. 4/17

WAR DIARY
or
INTELLIGENCE SUMMARY.
(Erase heading not required.)

Army Form C. 2118.

5th Bn. H.L.I.

Place	Date	Hour	Summary of Events and Information	Remarks and references to Appendices
ERBISOEUL	10.11.18		Protestant Church Parade 0.915. C. of E. 1015.	WX
			Comparative Strength Table	
			Strength as at 31/10/18. 2ND Officers. 4.11 OR.	
			Our Increase (a) details overleaf 18. 25.9	
			42. 670	
			Less Decrease (b) details overleaf 17. 144	
			25. Officers. 526 O.R.	WX
			Wm J__ Major	
			Comdg 1/5th H.L.I.	

WAR DIARY or INTELLIGENCE SUMMARY

Army Form C. 2118.

5th Bn. H.L.I.

(a) Increase:—

	Officers	O.R.	(b) Decrease:—	Officers	O.R.
1. From Hospital	2	74	1. To Hospital (Sick)	2	37
2. " Courses	—	33	2. " " (Wounded)	—	3
3. " Leave	8	143	3. " Courses	9	13
4. Reinforcements	6	7	4. " Leave	3	89
5. Detached	—	5	5. Detached	—	1
6. Miscellaneous	2	2	6. Left Battalion	2	—
	18	259	7. Miscellaneous	1	1
				17	144

Army Form C. 2118.

WAR DIARY
or
INTELLIGENCE SUMMARY.

5th Bn. H.L.I.

(Erase heading not required.)

Place	Date	Hour	Summary of Events and Information	Remarks and references to Appendices
			The following awards for valour were published during the month:— Medaille d'honneur avec Glaives en bronze. No. 200896 Pte. J Trowbridge.	

WAR DIARY
or
INTELLIGENCE SUMMARY.
(Erase heading not required.)

Army Form C. 2118.

B1   5th HLI

Place	Date	Hour	Summary of Events and Information	Remarks and references to Appendices
ERQUIGHEM	1/12/16		Battalion sent for training. "B" Coy attached to Battery. Demonstration by the 19th Battery R.F.A. the remainder of the Battalion practised rapid deployment.	
do	2/12/16		Training under Coy arrangements. A Coy at range B Coy working for 3 coys R.E.s, C Coy working party under R.E. B to 19th Battery R.F.A. 2/Lieut J.K. Chapman joined Battalion to reinforcement. 66 O.R.s joined as reinforcements.	✓
do	3/12/16		B Coy at range, A. C. & D Coys under Coy arrangements. the following officers attached temporarily to 19th Bty R.F.A. Lieut Marcola, Lieut the Turner 2/Lieut J Morrison, 2/Lieut W.J. Chapman, 2/Lieut W.R. Paire, 2/Lieut R. Leash, 2/Lieut J.S. Dick, 2/Lieut E.J. Brown, 2/Lieut L.M. Crea, 2/Lieut A. Wilson, 2/Lieut T. Cockburn All went to give 16 to 19th H.L.I. All other ranks joined the batteries as reinforcements.	✓
do	4/12/16		"B" and C Coy Training. A. Coy to 19th Battery R.F.A. remainder in ceremonial parade under Major Trotter. Major D.E. Broad regiment sent from Hospital. B Coy to 19th Batty R.F.A. Ept A Fulton rejoined Regiment from 9 to 9-45 from 10 to 11 weather. Coy arrangements R.S.M. McKean proceeds to U.K. on substitution leave. (contd)	✓

15 R
7 shots

WAR DIARY or INTELLIGENCE SUMMARY.

Army Form C. 2118.

(Erase heading not required.)

Place	Date	Hour	Summary of Events and Information	Remarks and references to Appendices
ERBISOEUL	6/10/18		C.S.M. D. Wilson appointed of R.S.M.	A/
do	7/10/18		Battalion & Coy Training. "B" Coy 19th Battery R.F.A.	
do			Battalion & Coy Training. "B" Coy Rapid Wiring. 2/Lieut W.S. Smith proceeded to 19th Battery R.F.A. for temporary attachment. The following Officers proceed to 1st Brigade Lewis Gun School at Hensies at present. 2/Lieut K.J. Chapman, 2/Lieut D.J. Somers & 2/Lieut K.J. Chapman	A/
do	8/10/18		C. Service, to Prestwein, or R.G. services	A/
do	9/10/18		Bn Training. Lt Col A. Crayford rejoins unit from Paris leave.	
do	10/10/18		Lt J.A. Porter is appointed Acid Commandant of ERBISOEUL. 2/Lt R.W. Jacob joins for duties attachment from R.F.A. The following Officers proceed U.K. to bring back the Colours of the Bn: Lieut P.S. Mellor, Lieut R. Leonbull, C.S.M. J. Graham, Sgt R. Hempel & Cpl J. Jacobs	A/
do	11/10/18		B" Coy. Demonstration for artillery on General Harrell. Lieut J. Sebbroel. B" Coy do.	A/
do	12/10/18		rejoined from Paris leave. Training under Coy arrangements.	A/
do	13/10/18		Training under Coy arrangement. Church Parade conducted by Lt Williams. R.C. members C.Q.M.S. J. Eakan, Sgt J. Burke, Cpl S. Jacobs proceed to U.K. to bring out Colours.	A/

WAR DIARY or INTELLIGENCE SUMMARY.

Army Form C. 2118.

(Erase heading not required.)

Place	Date	Hour	Summary of Events and Information	Remarks and references to Appendices
ERBISOEUL	14/12/16		Training under Coy arrangement.	
do	15/12/16		Battalion bathing at Baths at Coal Mines Colliery	A/
do	16/12/16		2nd Lieut A.J. Dicken proceeds 9th Bn. R.F.C. for one weeks attachment training under Coy arrangements. Lt. Col Cremming in confirms 2nd in Command of "A" Coy. C.O. Inspects "A" Coy	A/
do	17/12/16		Training under Coy arrangements. E Coy at range. C.O. Inspects "B" Coy	A/
do	18/12/16		Training under Coy arrangements. "D" Coy at range.	A/
do	19/12/16		Training under Coy arrangements. C.O. Inspects "C" Coy	A/
do	20/12/16		Battalion foremen Rev 2d.S. Duncan appointed controller of Lancaster. Lieut Corondell appointed Demobilization officer	A/
do	21/12/16		Interior economy by Coys. C.O. Inspects "D" Coy.	A/
do	22/12/16		Chur't services Vinschatricar 1000. Lof b. 0930. R6. 0930.	A/
do	23/12/16		Training under Coy arrangements. E.O. inspects Hqrs Coy. Capt Burns to return of the strength of the Battalion on being posted to the 12 th Bn. Royal Welsh	A/
do	24/12/16		Clothing issued to Coys. Coys carry out Bullding improvements. The following officers proceed to 157 Inf Brigade Lewis gun school at Chateau de	A/

Army Form C. 2118.

WAR DIARY
or
INTELLIGENCE SUMMARY.
(Erase heading not required.)

Place	Date	Hour	Summary of Events and Information	Remarks and references to Appendices
ERBISOEUL			Bussent 2/Lieut F. Morrison 2/Lt E.B. Smith 2/Lieut & Carr 2/Lieut A. Wilson, 2/Lieut C.M. West 2/Lt R.R. Vine 2/Lieut E. Jewell	W
do	25/10/18		Route day, no parades. The Divine Service Presbyterian 10.00 C of E 10.30 R.C. 10.30	W
do	26/10/18		Training under Coy arrangements. 2/Lt M.S. Devine proceeded to 1st Army	W
do	27/10/18		nil school at Harelbeke	
			Training under Coy arrangements. Lieut Horton R.G. proceeded to 1st Army	W
do	28/10/18		Musketry Training School Ostrenghen	W
			Training under Coy arrangements	W
do	29/10/18		Divine service Presbyterian service at 11.00, C of E at 09.00 R.C. at 10.00	W
do	30/10/18		"A" Ceremonial Parade	W
do	31/10/18		"B" Ceremonial Parade. Party which proceeded to U.K. for B[n] Colours returned with B[n] Colours	W

Army Form C. 2118.

BS S74/

WAR DIARY
or
INTELLIGENCE SUMMARY.
(Erase heading not required.)

Place	Date	Hour	Summary of Events and Information	Remarks and references to Appendices
			Officers O.Rs.	
			Strength at 30.11.17 42 715	
			Casualties as detailed overleaf 20 243	
			" " " " 62 958	
			Increase as detailed overleaf 22 117	
			40 841	
			Strength at 31.12.18	

Army Form C. 2118.

WAR DIARY
or
INTELLIGENCE SUMMARY
(Erase heading not required.)

Place	Date	Hour	Summary of Events and Information			Remarks and references to Appendices
				O.	O.R.	
ERBISŒUL			Conference Strength Statement for month			
			Inverse	O.	O.R.	
			from Ult. Leave	3. 55	30	
			" Rest Camp	2	1	
			" Junior Instr.	1 140		
			" From Course of Instruction			
			" Hospital	12 18	13 26	
			" Boys Bgn	1 23	1 29	
			" Local Leave	1 1	— 1	
			" Rest Camp	1	1	
			" Concentration Camp	1	5	
			" Boys Bgn	—	1	
			" D.A.D.S. XIII Corps	2	2	
			" Educational Classes	—	16	
				1	5	
			" Ult. for Concentration			
			Strength of Strength	3		
				20 243	22 117	

WAR DIARY
or
INTELLIGENCE SUMMARY.
(Erase heading not required.)

Army Form C., 2118.

Place	Date	Hour	Summary of Events and Information	Remarks and references to Appendices
			The following recommendations for awards were submitted.	
			Lt. /Qm. Cooper — Cross of France	M.S.M.
			Lt. W.F. Ayles — Military Medal 200016 Sgt. A. Powell	M.S.M.
			85802 Lt. W. Cumming 200120 Sgt. T.C. Cameron	do.
			Lt. J.W. Tart — Military Cross 200147 C.Q.M.S. F. Graham	do.
			do. 203223 Sgt. D. McKay	do.
			200861 R.Q.M.S. F. Chapman D.C.M. 200865 Sgt. J.A. Hamilton Austrian
			200296 C.Q.M.S. O.M. Kelly D.C.M. 201617 Sgt. N. Horton	do.
			200861 Sgt. F. Harries T.M. 201702 Sgt. A. Burton	do.
			210777 Sgt. L. Horton T.M. 332206 Sgt. H. McKay	do.
			200274 C.S.M. D. McLaren T.M. The following awards	
			201320 Sgt. J. Watson T.M. been granted	
			200230 C.S.M. J. Rogers M.S.M. 5982 Pte W. Mull	M.M.
			200384 C.Q.M.S. J. Graham do.	
			200271 C.Q.M.S. R. Vivash do.	
			200037 C.Q.M.S. A. Bain do.	
			200663 Sgt. A. Pitcairn do.	

WAR DIARY or INTELLIGENCE SUMMARY

Army Form C. 2118.

5th Bn. H.L.I.

Vol 10

Place	Date	Hour	Summary of Events and Information	Remarks and references to Appendices
ERBISOEUL	1/1/19		No training parades. Voluntary Divine Services. Special New Year dinner to NCOs & men by Companys, no accommodation being available to hold a Battalion dinner. Lieut J. Shedden proceeded to U.K. with party for demobilization & silence for 14 days leave. 9Lt P.R. Price was admitted to hospital from brigade Lewis Gun School.	
	2/1/19		Training under Company arrangements	Q/5M
	3/1/19		Brigade Ceremonial Parade on Great Parade Ground (K9d) under Brig. Gen. C.D. Hamilton Moore CMG DSO	Q/5M Ret US Q/5M
	4/1/19		Capt H.L. Wragham rejoined unit from UK leave. Training under Company arrangements. MO Lieut Nicholson and Lieut J.G. Mackenzie proceeded on three days leave to Brussels.	Q/5M
	5/1/19		Divine Service - Presbyterian Service taken by Rev Meaney and Rev Rankin of Marine Church Hut.	Q/5M

16 G
9 sheets

WAR DIARY
INTELLIGENCE SUMMARY.

Army Form C. 2118.

5th Bn. H.L.I.

1/2

(Erase heading not required.)

Place	Date	Hour	Summary of Events and Information	Remarks and references to Appendices
ERBISOEUL	6/1/19		Brigade Ceremonial Parade on Great Parade Ground (K9d)	
			"A" Coy proceeds to MONS on detachment to take over Guard duties from 7th H.L.I. at MONS Railway Station.	QMM
			Hired Telephone procured to PARIS. PLAGE Rest House.	QMM
	7/1/19		Training under Company arrangements	
	8/1/19		Training under Company arrangements. Brigade Paper Chase over 5 mile course.	QMM
			Major D.E. Bond DSO proceeded to 10th course at Senior Officers' School, Aldershot. Major W. Forbie assumed 2nd in Command of Bn.	QMM
	9/1/19		Ceremonial Parade on Great Parade Ground comprising 157th Inf Bde and civilian Inhabitants. Parade at which the Divisional Commander, Major General T.S. Marshall CMG. DSO. presented medal ribbons to NCO's & men of the Division. The following NCO's men of Bn were decorated:-	QMM
			MILITARY MEDALS	
			No 200846 Sgt S. Cook No 200377 Sgt S. Logan	
			No 200504 Sgt W. Stevenson No 201014 A/C L. Rae No 27648 L/C R. Lavin	
			No 200307 L/C G. Clark No 200524 Pte A. Robertson No 70056 Pte J. Alford	

Army Form C. 2118.

WAR DIARY
INTELLIGENCE SUMMARY.
(Erase heading not required.)

5th Bn. H.L.I.

Place	Date	Hour	Summary of Events and Information	Remarks and references to Appendices
ERQUELINNES	9/1/19		Presentation of Military Medal Ribbons (Continued)	
			No 203306 Pte C. L. Irvine No 202105 Pte C.P. Morgan	Appx
			No 200066 " J. Ross. No 58802 " N. Auld	Appx
	10/1/19		Training parade cancelled owing to baths at Coal Mines. GHQ letter allocated to the unit.	Appx
	11/1/19		Bn at disposal of OC Coys for interior economy and organisation	Appx
			Major W. Faulds proceeded to UK for demobilization	
			Capt R.H. Morrison M.C. assumed 2nd in Command of Bn.	
	12/1/19		Bathing at Coal Mines, GHQ. (Divine services cancelled)	Appx
			Lieut A.F.A. Wrigley joined the Bn. from 2nd Bn. H.L.I. & was posted to "A" Company	
	13/1/19		Training under Company arrangements. "B" Company under 2Lt R.C. King M.C. relieved "A" Company of Guard duties at HONS Railway Station. Lieut G. Cumming proceeded to UK on leave.	Appx
	14/1/19		Brigade Ceremonial Parade on Coal Parade Ground. To practise for the Corps Commander Review of the Division.	Appx

WAR DIARY
or
INTELLIGENCE SUMMARY.

Army Form C. 2118.

3rd H.L.I.

(Erase heading not required.)

Place	Date	Hour	Summary of Events and Information	Remarks and references to Appendices
FRBISCAL	15/4/19		Training under Coy arrangements	Q.M.
	16/4/19		Training under Coy arrangements. 2/Lt J Edward proceeded on Club leave. Lt J.S. Hilton took over the duties of Adjutant. 2/Lt J.K. Chapman proceeded to U.K. for demobilisation.	Q.M.
	17/4/19		Battalion Parade on Battalion Parade ground from 0900 till 1015 remainder of the morning under Coy arrangements	Q.M.
	18/4/19		Coys Commanders inspection of the lines in the Grand Parade ground. B.O.R. ribbons were presented to the following:— 200174 C.S.M George Murdoch, #16/7 Private Walter Gray, 85/170 Private William Jones, 10646 Private James Flemery. A concert was held by the John "C.B." Coy in Battalion concert Hall by the "B" Concert party. Lt Col A Crawford proceeded to Ayrshire on three days leave.	Q.M.
	19/4/19		Divine service instructions being taken by the Rev Chaney of the Western Division Unit.	Q.M.
	20/4/19		"B" Coy paraded to Brigade range and carried out the following practice:— 5 Round application & 10 Rounds Rapid (contd)	Q.M.

WAR DIARY
INTELLIGENCE SUMMARY

Army Form C. 2118.

Place	Date	Hour	Summary of Events and Information	Remarks and references to Appendices
ECKERSEUL	20/1/19		A draft of Infantry was held with the effected reference number of list of the following men 20985 L/Cpl T.R Passmore 20112 Pte A.C. Collinson 20048 Pte L Pearson 31185 Corpl J. Howard and 23234 Pte R.J Keller. The draft consisted of Lieutenant Capt H.L. Hooper, members being R. Nash, Hirst & Davis.	Appx
	21/1/19		Training under Coy arrangements. Rft. of 2 Lt Pearson attached to Headquarters as orderly officer. The Commander R.S.C. L.E. Commerford after	Appx
	22/1/19		B Coy so relieved to Coy of H.Q. at home orders in the list of companys Capt J. Foster proceeds to UK for Commission Board. Lieut & adj Cet the Battalion Hqrs. Cadre at Col W.E. Reynard returned from Brussels base.	Appx
	23/1/19		Training under Coy arrangements. Capt H.L. Hooper & Capt Newman proceed to Lunch on three days leave.	Appx
	24/1/19		Training under Coy arrangements to	Appx
	25/1/19		Training under Coy arrangements to Coy's Hqrs Sheet 22 of the defeat of	(cancel)

WAR DIARY
or
INTELLIGENCE SUMMARY.

(Erase heading not required.)

Army Form C. 2118.

Place	Date	Hour	Summary of Events and Information	Remarks and references to Appendices
ERBISŒUL	25/1/19		Battalion paraded for the purpose of proceeding to the battle fields of Waterloo.	A657M
	26/1/19		2 Officers and 100 O.R. proceeded. Divine Service. Instruction in to how to Honor. Capt L.P.H. Morrison M.C. proceeded to U.K. for Demobilisation.	A657M
	27/1/19		Training under Coy arrangements. 2/Lt W.E.C. Allen proceeded to Brussels on 10 days leave.	A657M
	28/1/19		Training under Coy arrangements. 2/Lt L.F.M. Clark proceeded to U.K.	A657M
			for Demobilisation.	
	29/1/19		Training under Coy arrangements. 9 Pte J. Wilson proceeded to U.K. for	A657M
			Demobilisation.	
	30/1/19		Training under Coy arrangements	A657M
	31/1/19		Training at disposal of Coy Commanders for interior economy & administration.	A657M

Army Form C. 2118.

WAR DIARY
or
INTELLIGENCE SUMMARY.
(Erase heading not required.)

1/7 15 H.T.9

Place	Date	Hour	Summary of Events and Information	Remarks and references to Appendices
ERQUISCOUL			Comparative Strength Statement for Month	
			Increase Off. O.R. Decrease Off. O.R.s	
			Hospital — 18 Hospital — 12	
			Leave 2 8 Leave 3 7	
			Course — 14 Course 1 1	
			Rest Camp 1 — Rest Camp 1 1	
			Reinforcements 1 4 Investigation — 20	
			Concentration Camp — 1 Guard of Strength 2 6	2000
			4 45 Educational Course — 16	
			Concentration Camp — 3	
			6 64	
			Demobilization 6 156	

WAR DIARY
INTELLIGENCE SUMMARY

Army Form C. 2118.

5/4/J

			Summary of Events and Information			Remarks and references to Appendices

Strength at 31/12/18   Officers   OR
                           40   841
         Increase   5   45
                          45   886
         Decrease   6   64
                          38   822   N5m

WAR DIARY
INTELLIGENCE SUMMARY.
(Erase heading not required.)

Army Form C. 2118.

1/9
5/4/19

Place	Date	Hour	Summary of Events and Information	Remarks and references to Appendices
			The following recommendations for awards were sent forward during the month.	9/5/1
			Mention in Cases Dispatch	
			R.A.M.S. Jamieson	
			C.Q.M.S. Graham B.	
			Sgt Samuel	
			Meritorious Service Medal	
			C.S.M. Angus	
			C.Q.M.S. Graham D	
			" Bain	

EXTRACTION SLIP

NO. .... SURNAME ....

CHRISTIAN NAMES ....

REGIMENT OR CORPS ....

EXTRACTED FOR:- ....
The Commanding Officer of the H.L.I. who were
relieved by 25th Nova Scotia Batt. at MŒUVRES
CANAL-DU-NORD in 1918.

2767/N H 11/60   DATE ....

2,090,212
  908,371
─────────
2,998,583
─────────

WAR DIARY
or
INTELLIGENCE SUMMARY.

Army Form C. 2118.

5th Bn. N.Z.I.

(Erase heading not required.)

Place	Date	Hour	Summary of Events and Information	Remarks and references to Appendices
ERBISOEUL	1/2/19	—	Training under Coy arrangements	
	2/2/19		Divine Service. Capt. J.W. Frew proceeded to U.K. for demobilization	
			Revd A.F.O. Whitfield resumed command of 19. Coy.	
	3/2/19		Training under Coy arrangements. Lieut S.M. Finan proceeded to U.K. for Demobilization.	
	4/2/19		Training under Coy arrangements. Lieut K.S. Wilson proceeded to Course at Oxford under Educational Scheme & 9/Lt G.S. Fish took over duties as acting adjutant. Lieut S.M. Downie reported from 1st Army School of Instruction etc. (Educational Course).	
	5/2/19		Training under Coy arrangements	
	6/2/19		Training under Coy arrangements. Lieut J. Cheeler proceeded to U.K. for demobilization	
	7/2/19		Training under Coy arrangements. Capt. H.L. Straghan proceeded to U.K. for demobilization	
			The following memo. was received from 1579th Inf. Bde. (Sgd):— "Refer on"	

17G
7 sheets

Army Form C. 2118.

WAR DIARY
or
INTELLIGENCE SUMMARY.
(Erase heading not required.)

5th Bn H.L.I.

Place	Date	Hour	Summary of Events and Information	Remarks and references to Appendices
ERBISOEUL	7/2/19		"Despatch as soon as possible following personnel aaa 10 Officers 200. O.R.s	
			"from 5th Bn H.L.I. to 3rd Bn H.L.I. 23rd Division aaa --- Officers were meant	
			"to either be volunteers for or compulsory returnable Army Occupation	
			"under P.O.14 of 29/1/19 aaa Officers to be Captains or Subalterns and from	
			"who have enlisted or wish to re-enlist under P.O.4 of Dec 1918 should be	
			"not to exceed aaa Same proportion of Corps, Corpls and H.Corpls to be	
			"included aaa two numbers you can despatch & probable date of departing aaa	
			Numbers were to 157 R.Os - 10 Officers and 180 O.Rs	B
			The Officers volunteering or detailed for the drafts were:-	
			Lieut J. Carmichael 250 N.C.	
			Lieut R.G. Morlan " R(obert) R. Loban	
			" H.D. Nicolson " S. Spence	
			" R. Park " J. Thompson	
			" R. Turnbull " J.C. Devane	
				" R. Erret.	
			The Operation Portable team of 5th H.L.I. was knocked out of 52nd Divn.	
			Completion in semi-final league cup 4th Royal Scots by 3 goals to 2	

WAR DIARY
INTELLIGENCE SUMMARY. 5th Bn. H.L.I.

Army Form C. 2118.

Place	Date	Hour	Summary of Events and Information	Remarks and references to Appendices
ERBISOEUL	9/2/19		Packing and cleaning up. Capt. P.C. KING proceeded to U.K. for demobilization.	B/
			Lieut A Penman joined Bn. on the disperse of 157th L.T.M.B.	
	9/2/19		Packing. Divine Service. Lieut J. Gilchrist rejoined from U.K. leave and resumed duties as Adjutant.	B/
	10/2/19		Training under Bn arrangements. Bathing. Lieut T.A. Aitken proceeded to U.K. for demobilization.	B/
	11/2/19		Training under Bn arrangements. Bathing. Lieut W. Cumming rejoined from U.K. leave.	B/
	12/2/19		Training. Bathing. Lt. Col. A. Crauford proceeded to Hospital + Lt. I. Carmichael took over Command of Bn. pending his return.	B/
	13/2/19		Training under Bn arrangements. 2/Lt. J.L. West proceeded to U.K. for demobilization.	B/
	14/2/19		Lieut W. Cumming proceeded to U.K. for demobilization.	B/
	15/2/19		2/Lt. J. Gow proceeded to U.K. for demobilization.	B/
	16/2/19		Divine Service. Lieut G.P. Ross, R.A.M.C. proceeded to join R.A.F. and Lt. Willis R.M.C. att. 6/H.L.B.K. took over his duties as Medical Officer of Bn.	B/
			Lt. Col. L. Carlisle, DSO joined Bn. and took over Command.	B/

WAR DIARY / INTELLIGENCE SUMMARY

Army Form C. 2118.

2/4 5th Bn H.L.I.

Place	Date	Hour	Summary of Events and Information	Remarks and references to Appendices
ENG/SOEUL	16/2/19		2nd Lieut G.S. Jack proceeded to U.K. on leave conducting duty and leave for 14 days leave.	B
	17/2/19		Lt Col R. Crawford reported from Hospital and 2nd Lieut L. Carlisle left for 4/6 W Smith & 4/6 GHS proceeded to BETHUNE to take over great order on railway from Spa Division.	B
	18/2/19			B
	19/2/19			
	20/2/19		Training under Coy arrangements	B
	21/2/19			
	22/2/19			
	23/2/19		Owing to the depletion of the Battalion through demobilisation the remnants were organized into two units (a) group for Army of Occupation under command of Lt Col R Crawford DSO MC and (b) Cadre and remaining men under command of Lieut BFA Whitfield. These two units were concentrated as far as possible into two separate large huts	B

Army Form C. 2118.

WAR DIARY
INTELLIGENCE SUMMARY.

5th Bn. H.L.I.

(Erase heading not required.)

Place	Date	Hour	Summary of Events and Information	Remarks and references to Appendices
ERBISOEUL	2/2/19		Training & reorganizing under Bgde arrangements.	B
	10/2/19		Training under Bgde arrangements. Lewis Gun training carried out by the Bngde.	B
	14/2/19		New to Lawson Cl. proceeds to join II Corps for Army of Occupation.	B
			XXII Corps Races took place near Free Forest MAZIERES	B
	22/2/19		63rd Divisl " do	B
	25/2/19		Training of draft under direction of O.C. draft. Wire from 157th Bde was received cancelling posting of draft for Army of Occupation. New orders read :- "Send 10 Officers and 80 O.Ranks other ranks and personnels over to 11th Royal Scots Fusiliers, 59th Division "Dunkirk".	
			General Remarks :- Owing to the rapidity of demobilization, classes formed under the Educational Scheme had to be more or less discontinued, except for occasional lectures. During the month everything possible was done to interest the NCOs & men in athletics.	B

WAR DIARY / INTELLIGENCE SUMMARY

5th Bn. 1421   2/6

The following is a comparative strength statement for the month:-

	Officers	O.Ranks
Strength as at 31st January 1919	38	822
Add Increase for month (Appendix A)	5	55
	43	877
Deduct Decrease for month (Appendix B)	20	325
Strength as at 28th March 1919	23	552

Appendix A (Increase)

	Officers	O.Ranks
From Course		1
" Hospital		
" A.C.C		
" XXII Corps Rein Camp	1	3
" U.K. Leave	2	3
" L.T.M.B	1	16
" 157 Bde. Hqrs		1
" D.A.P.M		1
" Taken on strength (Rein other)		1
" Remount Depot Le HAVRE		1
" D.A.O.S		
Total	5	55

Appendix B (Decrease)

	Officers	O.Ranks
To D.A.P.M		3
" XXII Corps Rein Camp		4
" Pos to Employment Coy		2
" No II Remount Depot LE HAVRE	1	
" 157th Bde Hqrs		2
" U.K. Leave	1	18
" Struck off strength	2	13
" Hospital	1	
" Courses	1	
" U.K. for Demobilization		
Army lists 140		567
Feb 2 367 144		
Total	20	552

WAR DIARY
INTELLIGENCE SUMMARY. 5th Br. M.I.

Army Form C. 2118.

2/7

Place	Date	Hour	Summary of Events and Information	Remarks and references to Appendices
			The following recommendations for awards were submitted during the month :- (Supplementary since Septr.)	
			Lieut W. Cumming recommended for M.C.	
			No 200463 R.Q.M.S G Ferguson " M.S.M	
			" 200681 L/C L Hamill " M.M.	
			Lieut J Leahurst " " Mentions	♂/
			No 200016 Sgt R. Bruce " "	
			" 200384 C.Q.M.S. J Graham " "	

WAR DIARY
or
INTELLIGENCE SUMMARY.
(Erase heading not required.)

Army Form C. 2118.

5th Bn. H.L.I.

WO/12

Place	Date	Hour	Summary of Events and Information	Remarks and references to Appendices
EDINBURGH	1/3/19		Lt. Col J. Crawford proceeded to Barracks on East Summer Time came into force at 2 a.m.	OL
	2/3/19		Divine service under Padre McGregor. Recreation trophies in the afternoon. Draft for Army of Occupation v "Cadre"	OL
				OL
	3/3/19		Training of Draft for Army of Occupation under orders of O.C. Drafts.	OL
	4/3/19		The G.O.C. 62nd Division inspected all Officers N.C.O.'s & men of the draft.	OL
			In the Army of Occupation.	OL
	5/3/19		Bathing & cleaning up.	OL
	6/3/19		Training of Draft under orders of O.C. Draft.	OL
	7/3/19		2/Lt N.S. Smith & L/6 O/Ranks rejoin from duty as Batmen.	
	8/3/19		The Draft for Army of Occupation received orders to proceed to Mons, undernoted Officers and 160 O/Ranks proceeded with the Draft.	
			LT. I. CARMICHAEL D.S.O. M.C. LT M.D. NICOLSON LT R. TURNBULL
			LT. R. PARK 2/LT E. GUEST	
	9/3/19		Divine Service.	OL
	10/3/19		Draft entrains at MONS.	OL

18 E
4 sheets

WAR DIARY or INTELLIGENCE SUMMARY

Army Form C. 2118.

5th Bn. H. L. I.

Place	Date	Hour	Summary of Events and Information	Remarks and references to Appendices
ERQUELINNES	11/3/19		2/LT G.S.DICK returns from Draft Conducting Duty	al
	12/3/19		Rifle Inspection in all Coys. Clearing Battalion Area	al
	13/3/19		Removing Q.M. Stores to MAZIÈRES	al
MAZIÈRES	14/3/19		Battalion moves to MAZIÈRES	al
	15/3/19		Commanding Officer inspects Billets & Battalion AREA	al
	16/3/19		Divine Service for Brigade under Padre McInnes. 2nd Lt W.S.SMITH proceeded to U.K. for demobilisation.	al
	17/3/19		Bathing. Lt L.S.HILLSON returns from Course at Oxford	al
	18/3/19		Rifle Inspection. Improving Battalion Area	al
	19/3/19		LT L.S.HILLSON and LT J.A.MORTON proceed to U.K. for demobilisation	al
	20/3/19		LT. A. PERMAN (LTM.B.) proceeded to join Cadre at NOYELLES	al
			LT R.G. MORTON transferred to U.K. under instructions from the War Office (3rd A'+ S H)	al
			LT J. STEWART attd BDE H.Q° proceeded to U.K. for demobilisation.	al
SOIGNIES	21/3/19		Battalion moves to SOIGNIES. 4/LT B. SPROUL proceeded on leave to UK	al
	22/3/19		2/LT G.S. DICK proceeded to U.K. for demobilisation. Two Rank out in Q.M. Stores	al
			As a result of which 5 O/Ranks were admitted to Hospital	al

WAR DIARY or INTELLIGENCE SUMMARY.

Army Form C. 2118.

5th Bn. H.L.I.

Place	Date	Hour	Summary of Events and Information	Remarks and references to Appendices
SOIGNIES	22/3/19		Royal Engineer Officer inspects damage caused by fire on 22/3/19	A
	24/3/19		The undernoted Officers and 1 Other proceed to join 9th Bn. (S.W.) H.L.I.	A
			2/Lt R. GRAHAM, 2/Lt J. MORRISON, 2/Lt D.G. OWENS, 2/Lt J.R. McLUNG	A
	25/3/19		Court of Enquiry held on fire in O.M. Stores on 22/3/19	A
	26/3/19		Parade classes at kit inspection and preparing kits for inspection	
	27/3/19		Proceeding of Court to follow	
	28/3/19			A
	29/3/19		2/Lt H.S. DOWNIE proceeds to XXII Corps Camp for duty	
			Information received from 139 Bde that the identity of S/Lt to 7th Bn L.I is to be preserved.	A
	30/3/19		Divine service in SPION CE HAYNE SOIGNIES.	A
	31/3/19		Inspection of Cadre by C.O.	A
			Strength of Unit as at 29th February 1919 Officers 23 O.Ranks 325	
			" " " " 31st March 1919 " " " " 48.	A

Army Form C. 2118.

WAR DIARY
or
INTELLIGENCE SUMMARY. 5th Bn. N.Z.I.

(Erase heading not required.)

Place	Date	Hour	Summary of Events and Information	Remarks and references to Appendices
	3/4		The following Recommendations for Awards were submitted during the month :- (Roumanian Decorations).	
			1. Major D.E. Brand DSO. recommended for Officier, Star of Roumania	
			2. Lieut L. W. Ross " " Chevalier, Star of Roumania	
			3. Capt. K. H. Morrison M.C. " " Chevalier, Order of Mihaiu 3rd Cl.	
			4. R.S.M.S. G. Jennison (No 20046¹) " " Medaille Barbate ei Credinta 1st Cl.	
			5. No 20027u C.S.M. D. McLaren " do 2nd Cl	
			6. " 55970 Pte O. Jones DCM " do 3rd Cl	
			7. " 416.17 " to Gray DCM " do "	
			8. " 40606 " J. Fleming DCM " do "	
			9. " 43247 Cpl 9396 D.F. Hunter V.C. " Croix de Virtute Militara 2nd Cl.	
			10. " 20081 L/c B. Humier " do	A
			31.3.19.	Ahansford Lt Col Comdg 1/5th H.L.I.

To 52nd Division

Attached A.F.C. 2118
received from 5 K.L.I.
is passed to you please

Russell
Lieut
a/Bde Major
157th Bde.

H.Q.
157TH INFANTRY
BRIGADE.
No. 187/45
Date 8/6/19

To 157th Inf. Bde.

Herewith War Diary of 1/8th Bn. H.L.I. for months of April & May — till date of arrival at Gailes.

Please acknowledge receipt.

Jas Gilchrist Lt & Adjt.
1/8th Bn H.L.I.

30/5/19.

WAR DIARY
INTELLIGENCE SUMMARY.
(Erase heading not required.)

Army Form C. 2118.

5th Br. 17.1.

Place	Date	Hour	Summary of Events and Information	Remarks and references to Appendices
BOGNIES	5/4/19	—	Daily rifle inspections. Cleaning rifles etc	
	6/4/19		Church Parade for Cadre of the Division	
	7/4/19		7/Lt M.P. Dawrie proceeded on leave from HONS CADRES leaving Calais 7/4/19	
	8/4/19		Kit rifle inspections. inspection of Billets	
	12/4/19		Lieut A. Penman 9th HLI. (attached HL Chinese Labour Corps NOYELLES) relation on returning to us from 13/3/19.	
	13/4/19		Church Parade.	
	14/4/19		Boxing at Divisional Baths.	
	15/4/19		Inspection of Arms & equipment by Lt-Col Crawford	
	16/4/19		Party of 1 officer + 8 O/R proceeded by Motor Lorry to visit Battle.	
	17/4/19		5th HLI Cadre Association Football Team played 527 Fld RFA in 52nd Divl Cadre Association Cup. — Result after extra time draw.	
	18/4/19		Replay of Association match — Result 3 goals to nil (against 5/HLI)	
	19/4/19		Capt I.M. L. Coghlan proceeded to UK on special leave. General Lindsay decided to Brunier from 12.00 today till 0700 on 22nd inst.	
	20/4/19		Voluntary Church Service	

Army Form C. 2118.

WAR DIARY
or
INTELLIGENCE SUMMARY.

1st Bn. M.I.   HQ

(Erase heading not required.)

Place	Date	Hour	Summary of Events and Information	Remarks and references to Appendices
SOIGNIES	23/4/19		2/Lt H.S. Jerome rejoined Hdqrs. Crs from U.K. leave.	—
	24/4/19		Warning Order received re entrainment.	—
	25/4/19		Capt L. Laflin rejoined from U.K. leave.	—
	28/4/19		Battalion commenced loading vehicles at 1000. Bn. entire entrained at Soignies & left for DUNKIRK at 1800.	—
DUNKIRK	29/4/19		Arrived Dunkirk 1200. Vehicles were off loaded & taken on quay side.	—
	30/4/19		Personnel detrained & ——. Lined aides on vehicles.	—

Army Form C. 2118.

WAR DIARY
~~INTELLIGENCE~~ SUMMARY.

5th Bn H.L.I.

(Erase heading not required.)

Instructions regarding War Diaries and Intelligence
Summaries are contained in F. S. Regs., Part II.
and the Staff Manual respectively. Title pages
will be prepared in manuscript.

Place	Date	Hour	Summary of Events and Information	Remarks and references to Appendices
DUNKIRK	3/5/19		Loaded vehicles on board SS "VIRGATCH" & sailed 1200. arriving SOUTHAMPTON	
SOUTHAMPTON	4/5/19	0800	at 0800	
	4/5/19		Entrained for GAILES after transferring vehicles at 2000.	
	5/5/19	1800	Arrived GAILES 1800.	

www.ingramcontent.com/pod-product-compliance
Lightning Source LLC
Chambersburg PA
CBHW081401160426
43193CB00013B/2080